A MINDFULNESS TEACHER'S HANDBOOK

*Surprise your students
not just by what you teach
but by how you teach*

Suryacitta

(The Happy Buddha)

© Copyright 2019

Suryacitta

The right of Suryacitta to be identified as the author of this work has been asserted by him in accordance with the Copyright, Designs and Patents Act 1998.

All rights reserved. No reproduction, copy or transmission of this publication may be made without express prior written permission. No paragraph of this publication may be reproduced, copied or transmitted except with express prior written permission or in accordance with the provisions of the Copyright Act 1956 (as amended). Any person who commits any unauthorised act in relation to this publication may be liable to criminal prosecution and civil claims for damage.

Although every effort has been made to ensure the accuracy of the information contained in this book, as of the date of publication, nothing herein should be construed as giving advice. The opinions expressed herein are those of the author.

ISBN: 978-1-093564-26-6

CONTENTS

page

	About the book	1
	About the author	2
1	COMMON MISTAKES	5
	Too much information	6
	Too much explanation	7
	Talking about New York is not New York	9
	Try to be more mindful	9
	Mindfulness will make you feel good	11
2	THE THREE PILLARS OF MINDFULNESS TEACHING	13
	Simple	14
	Elegant	16
	Practical	17
3	THE MINDFULNESS JOURNEY	20
	Melting ice cubes	21
	Becoming mushy	22
	Discovering where we are	23

page

4	ALLOWING SILENCE TO BE THE TEACHER	25
	Silence	26
	Pauses	28
	Un-minding	30
5	WATCHING THOUGHTS	32
	The clicky pen	34
	Becoming aware of thinking	35
	Labelling thoughts	36
	The fuel and the fire	38
	The thought buses	39
6	GUIDING MEDITATIONS	41
	Introducing a meditation	42
	The Mindfulness of Breathing meditation	43
	Ending a meditation	45
	The Being at Home meditation	46
	The Compassion meditation	49
	A meditation on vulnerability	52
	The Just Sitting meditation	54
	Guiding other meditations	57
7	ENQUIRY: TRUSTING SIMPLICITY	58
	The purpose of enquiry	59
	Preparing for the enquiry	61
	Opening the enquiry	62
	Doing the enquiry	63
8	DANCING WITH DRAGONS	66
	Your secret practice	67
	Two pools of practice	69

		page
	The Dancing with Dragons meditation	71
	Idiot compassion and challenging your students	73
	Working with difficult emotions and pain	75
	Being honest with ourselves	77
9	GOING BEYOND CLICHES	79
	Acceptance	80
	Let go	82
	Is that so?	84
	Sit with it	85
	Be kind to yourself	86
10	TEACHING INTUITIVELY	90
	Accessing your intuition	91
	Tuning in to your intuition	92
	Keeping it simple, elegant and practical	96
	The benefits of intuitive teaching	98
11	USING STORIES AND METAPHORS	101
	Stories	102
	Texting and nexting	102
	Grandmother mind	104
	Metaphors	107
	Mirror in the bathroom	107
	A room with two doors	109
	Fiddling with the flowers and standing back	111

page

12 MORE STORIES AND METAPHORS — 114
- Gulliver's travels — 114
- The two arrows — 115
- The seventy-seven problems — 117
- Who's this in the shower with me? — 118
- The river — 120
- The meditation master and the cleaning lady — 122
- The drunk and the moon — 124
- Johnny and the biscuit tin — 125
- Bursting balloons — 125

13 AN EIGHT-WEEK COURSE IN MINDFULNESS AND COMPASSION — 128
- Week 1 The jewel in the ice — 129
- Week 2 The feeling body — 130
- Week 3 Living in the present moment — 131
- Week 4 Calming the chattering mind — 133
- Week 5 Dancing with dragons — 137
- Week 6 The ABC of mindfulness — 139
- Week 7 Compassion — 141
- Week 8 Bringing mindfulness to life – and what next? — 143

Further resources — 146

Acknowledgement — 148

Contact Suryacitta — 150

About the book

Please read this book with your heart, your intuition, and not with your head. I do not like over-explaining things. I prefer to leave people to do a little intuitive work themselves. Not having everything explained means that we can grow into understanding, rather than waiting like baby birds for every morsel of information to be fed to us.

This is not an academic approach, but I believe academics could benefit from reading it. It is not intended to be a thorough critique of mindfulness teaching but a collection of reflections from my own experience of teaching it, and of teaching others to teach it. The book is sprinkled with stories and metaphors which you can use or adapt.

The book can be read from front to back or just dipped into. If I have done my job well, you should find something useful on every page.

Please use anything from this book which will help you in your teaching. You may need to change some of the ideas and teachings in this book depending on your client group. However, I believe the principles always remain the same.

About the author

Mindfulness is now being taught in so many ways, in so many settings and by many different people. To me it is something beautiful. I have dedicated my life to its practice since 1989, and this book has come out of my own practice and teaching over the past thirty years.

From 1989 I practised mainly with the help of books I came across. I seemed to find just the right book at just the right time. I shared meditation with friends, some of whom benefitted themselves and still practise to this day. In 1993 I went to the Glastonbury music festival, came across a Buddhist group running meditation sessions there, and learned a little more about meditation. After another year practising alone I became involved with a Buddhist organization, and in 1999 on a four-month retreat in Spain I was ordained and given the name Suryacitta - he who has a heart like the sun.

From 2001 to 2005 I lived in a Buddhist retreat centre dedicated to a life of meditation and silence. It was a wonderful period, of which you can read more on my website suryacitta.com. Towards the end of my time there I knew that this practice was for everybody, not just Buddhists or people living quiet lives in the mountains.

I then moved to Brighton where I met Gaynor, who had just taken up meditation and would later become my wife. Whilst in Brighton I began running courses on happiness at a local arts centre, and also retreats and courses on Buddhism and meditation at Brighton Buddhist Centre.

In 2008 we moved to Leicestershire to be near Gaynor's family, and for the next four years I continued to run meditation courses. I knew all along that teaching mindfulness and Buddhism was the only thing I wanted to do, and in 2012 Gaynor and I set up Be Mindful Now CIC, a non-profit company offering mindfulness retreats and courses throughout the UK.

As our reputation grew we started getting invited to Europe and Australia to run events there. We continue to run courses and retreats, and have since extended into providing mindfulness training in the workplace, particularly in the healthcare and business sectors. Alongside this we also offer mindfulness teacher training programmes to people who are interested in teaching mindfulness as a career and to those who wish to bring it into the workplace.

I have published three previous books on mindfulness: *Happiness and How it Happens: Finding Contentment Through Mindfulness* (2011), *Mindfulness and Compassion: Embracing Life with Loving-Kindness* (2015) and *A Mindful Life: Who's this in the shower with me? How to get out of your head and start living* (2017).

I was moved to write the book you are now reading because I see at first hand, via the training retreats we run at Be Mindful Now CIC, the difficulties and challenges teachers of mindfulness face. I also see some of the more experienced teachers struggling to communicate the subtleties of this ancient and beautiful practice.

When I am teaching, I often use the image of a jewel to illustrate mindfulness. A jewel has many facets; you turn the jewel a fraction and there is another facet, shimmering right at you. When running a course or a series of workshops, what we are really doing is exploring the jewel of mindfulness, or awareness as it is also called. It is something we explore for the rest of our lives if we commit ourselves to it.

1 COMMON MISTAKES

"Mindfulness is not educational, but transformational."
Chogyam Trungpa

This chapter explores some common approaches to mindfulness teaching and advocates some different ones. It initially explores giving the right amount of information to our students and how to pace our teaching; it is important to teach at a pace which allows the students to absorb what is being taught. It also suggests that we need to give our students information that has an impact on them, that makes a difference to their lives, and not just information for the sake of it.

Another area of exploration within this chapter is the type of language we use to our students. This will influence the approach that students adopt towards their practice, so it is essential to use wise and helpful language from the beginning. Lastly it looks at mindfulness not being a quick fix, in fact not being a fix at all but more like medicine which, taken over time, helps us be well.

Too much information

One of the most common mistakes I find in mindfulness teaching is that of teachers giving too much information. On our courses we always say early on that this course is not about information. I often illustrate this with the use of an old vinyl LP record.

I hold up a vinyl LP and ask people if they know what this is. They all do, even the younger students. I ask them what happens when they put the needle onto the record. Some say it crackles, which is true. However, my point is that nothing happens for a few seconds - there is a pause, a gap, just silence. This happens several times between the tracks - there is a pause, then the next track plays. Then we turn over the record and the same thing happens - there is music, then there is a pause. When CDs came out in the 1980s, I remember thinking to myself that the gaps and pauses between the tracks were shorter. However, I didn't think I was on to anything significant at the time.

Now we have digital music, without gaps and pauses, without silence between the tracks. Each track goes straight into the next one without a break, like tumbling dominoes. This, I suggest, represents a wider change in our lives as a whole. They are filled with activity and our minds are filled with thoughts and ideas. We live without pauses, we live without silence, and as a culture we are paying the price.

I tell our students that this course is going to be more like a vinyl LP record than a digital download. We are going to have pauses and silence.

I will not fill my students' heads full of words and information. This is not what mindfulness is about. We do of course have to give some information, but the information we give needs to be digestible and not lead them into more mind games and intellectualisation. I prefer to give a little information that has an impact, rather than to overload the student with lots of facts and ideas.

Too much explanation

Recently, during a supervision on a mindfulness teacher training course, one of my student teachers said that two people in her group had announced that they just didn't get it, and that she had tried to explain further to them what "it" was. This, I said to her, was understandable but a missed opportunity.

Instead of launching into more conceptual explanations of mindfulness during the supervision, I asked her to feel her contact with the chair she was sitting on. "Now what is there to get or not get about that?" I asked. She couldn't say anything for a few seconds. She just shook her head and said, "So simple." Those two words were music to my ears.

Simplicity takes us out of the pressure cooker of over-explaining, into the here and now of direct experience. It is very easy to think that we have to explain everything. We don't. In that moment of my taking her into her direct experience, she moved out of her head and into her experience of the body in the present moment. She became curious. We cannot be curious and lost in our heads at the same time.

It is common to have the view that if we understand mindfulness like we understand chemistry or a road map then we will know what it is and we can move on to the next thing. Mindfulness is not something to be understood; it is something to be practised, something to feel. Mindfulness, or awareness as I often call it, is what we sense the world with.

It is not that we never discuss mindfulness conceptually, not that we never study it, but that we always need to come back to the simplicity of this very moment, which takes no thinking about. This is why a lot of us find it difficult; we want to think about it, we want to tear it apart and analyse it. But mindfulness is *knowing* that I want to tear it apart, that I want to analyse it, and then consciously letting go of this thought and impulse and returning to the present moment.

The problem is that we don't trust this simple knowing. Surely there is more to it than this, we think.

My job as a teacher is to keep mindfulness just out of the reach of people's intellect. There is a saying in Zen Buddhism: "*neti neti*". It translates as something like: "not this, not that, and not that either". We can come to mindfulness and try to pin it down with a definition or a simplistic explanation; we want to know it. But mindfulness is not a thing; awareness is not an object. It doesn't have a colour or a shape or any obvious material qualities. Just like space, it exists not as a thing itself but as a medium which allows other things to appear.

This is why avoiding the temptation to over-explain can be so helpful to students. It gives them the opportunity to sense into their awareness of the moment, to feel their way into mindfulness, to use their intuition rather than their intellect.

Talking about New York is not New York

This metaphor is one I sometimes share to illustrate the difference between thinking and direct experience. If you want to know what New York is like you can ask people about it. You can look at pictures of all the famous streets, get excited reading about the Statue of Liberty, and imagine eating a pizza on Fifth Avenue.

However, all this reading, talking and dreaming is not New York; it is all in your mind. Of course, that is not a reason not to read about it or get excited about going, but it is not a direct experience of New York. To get the experience of New York, you need to go there yourself.

In the same way, all the information we give about mindfulness is not mindfulness. It can help to come to a relative understanding, but it can just as easily give people a false understanding of what it is.

Try to be more mindful

Perhaps another error we can easily fall into is to ask students to be more mindful during the day, or to try just a little harder. I think this is very misleading language and could lead students into an over-calculated approach to mindfulness practice. It is easy to think that mindfulness or awareness is something that we need to get, we need to develop. We can talk about it in this way but it is neither accurate nor helpful.

Try this: Stop being aware right now for ten seconds. Impossible, isn't it? So if we cannot stop being aware, or being mindful, then there is no need to ask our students to try to be more mindful. Mindfulness or awareness - I will use these terms interchangeably - is already here. It is here on the basis of our being human.

Trying doesn't work because awareness is already here. So we don't ask people to try and be more mindful. If we do, it just generates a very subtle but pernicious tension. It actually takes us away from relaxing into the present moment.

Instead of asking our students to be more mindful, we can ask them to notice what takes them away from being mindful, from being present in their own lives. For example, if they are doing the ironing or washing the car, instead of trying to be mindful we can simply ask our students to notice what takes them away from the activity, and it is always thinking.

On our courses and retreats we really just ask people to notice what takes them away from the here and now, to become aware of the thoughts that have hijacked their mind and taken it off to something that happened yesterday, or that might happen tomorrow. Having become aware of those thoughts they can then let them go, by the simple expedient of returning to the present moment and refocusing on what is actually happening - the feelings in the body, the movement of the breath, the sounds around them.

Mindfulness will make you feel good

Another problem we can run into as teachers is that for most people mindfulness isn't always pleasant, and in today's world we want pleasure. Most of us would not want to bow down in front of a Buddha image or any other image for that matter. I have no problem myself as I am a Buddhist and I see the point of it. But each and every one of us bows down a number of times a day to our cultural gods - security, comfort and pleasure. We try to engineer our lives so that we never have to have any unpleasantness, but of course it doesn't work.

When students come to a mindfulness course they will if they are honest enough admit that they want to feel better, and there is nothing wrong with that. I think a lot of teachers want to make their students feel better too, and again there is nothing wrong with that. However, to feel good, at least in the short term, is not what mindfulness is really about.

It is true that we are likely to feel better after practising regularly for a time, but there is no guarantee. We are releasing a lot of repressed and unacknowledged emotions from the past, so there are going to be times when things are difficult. When asked about this I sometimes give a conceptual explanation, but I think there is a different approach that often makes more sense to students and encourages them to continue.

I will tell them that mindfulness is like medicine. When I was a young boy my mum would take me to the doctor when I had a bad cough, or earache or whatever it was that was troubling me. The doctor would give my mum medicine to help cure me of the ailment. The medicine did not always taste nice, but it invariably made me well.

Mindfulness is similar; it does not always feel good and pleasant, but it makes us well. It is medicine for the mind. The Buddha is known to Buddhists as the mind's physician. We live in a world where we want the instant fix, but our work as teachers is to show that this approach is actually part of the problem and not the solution.

2 THE THREE PILLARS OF MINDFULNESS TEACHING

"As long as we live or as long as we have this body, it is not possible to get out of suffering. So the point is how to change our suffering into the true joy of life. This is how to help others."

Suzuki Roshi

Mindfulness has to make a difference to a person's life, so our teaching must be carried out with that primary aim in mind. This chapter considers the fundamental qualities of effective mindfulness teaching, the "three pillars" on which I believe our teaching needs to be based.

The first is that our teaching should be simple, in that we should always attempt to make mindfulness accessible and easy to understand for our students. The second, which may surprise you, is that our teaching should be elegant, in that it should be uncluttered and free from superfluous words and ideas. In the words of Charlotte Joko Beck, elegance is achieved not just by what you say, but by what you don't say. The third is that our teaching should be practical, in that it should be relevant to everyday life and equip our students with tools and strategies that they can use and apply in all areas of their lives.

Simple

The word "simple" means easily understood, presenting little difficulty, not elaborate. So our teaching needs to convey the simplicity of mindfulness and the practising of it. To me, sharing mindfulness should be uncomplicated.

Most teachers I see are sincere, honest and conscientious but in my view they frequently over-complicate mindfulness. They rely far too much on words. Most say far more than they need to and often lose their students in the jungle of ideas and concepts.

Simplicity is where the power is. If you want to reach more people, it's not theory and complexity they are after. We need to keep in touch with the essence of what we are sharing with our students; otherwise it becomes just a lot of words and ideas. I think it is very easy as teachers to give lots of handouts. To some this looks impressive, but it has never impressed me. We do give handouts on our courses but we keep them to a minimum. We don't want to encourage our students to think they will find what they are looking for in handouts.

At the beginning of our courses we tell our students that each of them will leave this course with less than they came with: less anxiety, less stress, less judgment, less worry, and just as importantly they should leave with fewer ideas. Remember that in mindfulness we are not looking for answers.

When I teach, I do so from the position of simplicity. Rather than debate with a student the meaning of this word or that phrase, I often bring them back to awareness, and the awareness that this thought, this intention to find the right answer, arises and then will pass away. Then something else will enter into their experience - a sound, a thought, a bodily sensation, a perception.

The point is to show students that we are not trying to work something out or to understand mindfulness intellectually. We are rather developing an attitude and practice of knowing and feeling what we are experiencing in each present moment as it passes.

Although our minds like to complicate things, being aware is very simple. Right now be aware of your contact with the chair you are sitting on, the sound of distant traffic, or seeing these words before your eyes. This is awareness.

Mindfulness is not philosophy; it is not a theory about life but a practice which transforms the individual. So the information which we share needs to assist in this transformation. Theory and complexity can just get in the way.

For me, keeping teaching and practice simple is magical. It is thrilling because it enables me to prevent students from intellectualising mindfulness. It excites me because I see that when somebody moves out of their head, from trying to understand mindfulness and into an experience of mindfulness itself, it has an impact, and then the transformation begins. It is absolutely wonderful to see this happen.

Elegant

In my dictionary "elegance" means stylishness, and it also means beauty that shows unusual effectiveness and simplicity. To teach elegantly is to communicate with clarity, in a way that is uncluttered with jargon and clichés.

Elegant teaching is often about knowing when not to say something, to be quiet. Pausing when we teach is a wonderful way of taking people out of their heads and back into their present experience. Elegance is about what we leave out rather than what we put in. An elegant woman knows what *not* to wear. A gorgeous Zen garden is elegant because it is uncluttered.

Be wary of cluttering your students' minds with too much theory, too many ideas and even your own beliefs. Can we have the courage just to pause quietly when they are expecting the answer to their question, or the next mouthful of information? This is very daring and can be exhilarating for both teacher and student at the same time.

Sometimes, instead of answering a question, a little smile may be more effective, or a raised eyebrow or a shrug of the shoulders.

Elegance is knowing how and when to use stories, images, and metaphors. Often in our classes, after sharing a story or a metaphor, we will fall quiet and the students are then allowed to digest what has just been said.

Elegance also brings beauty to the journey. Although on a mindfulness course we spend a lot of time looking at how we suffer, we also need to show our students that there is a way out of it. This is where beauty comes in. I always start my courses with beauty, a glimpse of the jewel of joy which is already shining within their hearts, but dusted over with years of neglect, much like the sun always continuing to shine even when it is covered by clouds. My purpose is to show each student how to clear away the clouds of anxiety, worry, guilt or self-obsession, and allow the jewel of joy to shine in his or her life once more.

Practical

My dictionary defines "practical" as being concerned with the actual doing of something rather than with ideas and theory. Keeping our teaching practical means that it should relate to real situations and be relevant to our students' experience of everyday life.

Our purpose is to show each person who walks through that door how they create their own suffering and how they can stop doing it, or at the very least do less of it. Our work as teachers is not about us, not about being liked. It is easy to see niceness as being kindness and compassion, but it is not. True compassion can be very practical, and in the context of teaching it is being willing to challenge people and to wake them up out of their suffering. If you are willing to challenge your students and not make it all nice and woolly, they will be forever grateful to you, even if at first they may resist it.

When we are teaching, we need to know who is teaching. What I mean is that there is no place for the people pleaser, and we all have a people pleaser inside. The people pleaser needs to step aside and allow our clarity and simplicity to do the teaching.

Keeping mindfulness teaching practical means we keep it grounded and ensure that the points we make are relevant to the real lives of our students. It means the ideas and tools we share with them can be used and applied in their relationships - at work, with friends and in every other area of their lives.

For example, it is very easy to say to our students that they should let go of thoughts when they are caught up in some drama in their heads. However, it is far more effective to give them a practical tool to help them to do this. Instead of just vaguely asking them to let go of thoughts we can show them how to observe a thought, label it as a thought and so divest it of its power.

When our students are struggling with difficult emotions, we can share some practical ways of gaining a perspective on the issue. We can show them how to befriend the difficult emotion and how to avoid fuelling the drama.

In my view there is nothing wrong with ideas and theory in the right context, and sometimes it can be very helpful and stimulating to engage with them. But when we are guiding students along the path to mindfulness as a practice, it is far more important to connect clearly and directly with the present moment experience and their everyday lives.

*

We don't want to be teaching mindfulness as if it is just another subject to study. To teach with simplicity and elegance takes courage, but when we do this it is effective and makes a practical difference to our students' lives. It comes from our heart and goes straight to the heart of the student. It moves them, it stirs them, but most of all it changes them.

3   THE MINDFULNESS JOURNEY

"When we protect ourselves so we won't feel pain, that protection becomes like armour, like armour that imprisons the softness of the heart."

Pema Chodron

When beginning a course, a retreat or a series of workshops, I like to set the scene for the journey of mindfulness for the students. Even if it is one-to-one work then I still offer this as a way of looking at what we are engaged in. This chapter offers one possible way of setting the scene.

As mentioned earlier, I like to begin by telling new students that they will leave with less than they came with. In this world of "you pay something and you get something in return" it often raises a few eyebrows. I like to see raised eyebrows; it means I have touched on something. This may be the first challenge, and I am here to challenge my students, as kindly as I can.

Melting ice cubes

The first week of our course is called "The jewel in the ice". In outlining the mindfulness journey, I like to blend the image of a jewel with the lovely metaphor of melting ice cubes from Charlotte Joko Beck's wonderful book, *Nothing Special*.

Imagine each human being is like a block of ice, an ice cube, with little legs and arms sticking out. This is the human being most of the time. This ice cube has in its centre a beautiful, glittering, shining jewel. This jewel represents the jewel of a life of joy, a life of contentment or less stress - whatever term does it for you.

But the beautiful jewel is inside this block of ice and we don't have access to it - although we know it exists, or we wouldn't bother trying to do something about it.

The ice is created primarily out of fear, out of our rigidly held beliefs such as: I need to be right, life has to go my way, life should not be painful, s/he should not do that, and so on.

We go about our life as this ice cube hoping that when we bump and slide into another person they will shatter before we do, because we are scared of our own vulnerability. Ice cubes hurt; they have a hard time because they have sharp edges which are easily knocked and chipped.

Because we are frozen we have no water to drink so we are thirsty most of the time. Yet we don't really know what we are thirsty for. We may soften a little at parties, but the underlying tension remains and the softening is temporary.

Becoming mushy

So how do we gain access to the jewel at the centre of this block of ice? Well of course, we melt the ice. If you put ice in the sun it just melts. Mindfulness is like the sun. If we know how to bring the sun of mindfulness and shine it on our own ice cube-ness, we can start the process of melting the ice. We soften a little. In the words of Charlotte Joko Beck, we start to become mushy. The journey of mindfulness is to become mushier and mushier.

If you leave an ice cube in the sun for long enough the melting doesn't stop. The ice just continues to melt, and in the end it becomes a puddle. So gradually in the months, years and decades of practice, we move from being an ice cube to becoming a puddle. How is that for a vision of the future?

I love to see people's faces at this point, as it is the last thing they are expecting. They are fully expecting a conceptual explanation of mindfulness but they don't get one yet - that will come later. For now, what they get is a vivid image of themselves as a puddle, which grabs their attention and curiosity.

Back to the image of the ice. What melts the ice is our own ability to observe ourselves both in meditation and in daily life. Self-observation is the sun which melts the ice. This self-observation is made of honesty and curiosity.

What also melts the ice is when we meet a puddle, or in other words somebody who is mushier than we are. So hopefully as a teacher you will help to melt the ice cube-ness of your students.

As the melting gets underway we begin to sense the jewel at the centre of all this. We may begin to feel a little less anxiety, a little more ease in our life. We may notice we are less neurotic, and we worry a little less. This is the emerging of the jewel. We cannot gain access to this jewel without some melting taking place.

At the same time as melting the ice around the jewel, our practice helps us to see how we create the ice with our self-centred thinking. As a consequence, this prevents us from creating more ice each and every day.

So as teachers our work is to help our students become mushier and mushier as their practice continues.

Discovering where we are

However, it is not a journey without upset. The melting of the ice can bring both joy and tears, but both are part of the process of the softening of our deeply held emotions and rigidly held beliefs that create bodily tension and mental stress.

I always point out that each moment of honest observation of how we are, each moment of feeling and experiencing the body without the mental storyline, is a moment of melting. We don't have to try to melt the ice; it just happens whenever we are willing to come into the present moment and to experience ourselves as we are.

Then those small cracks, those little changes begin to appear in our lives and they create more encouragement to continue the journey, a journey which isn't a journey to anywhere else, but where we have been all this time but never noticed. In other words, it is a journey of discovering ourselves and life as it really is and has been all the time.

In my experience one of the benefits of illustrating the mindfulness journey in this way is that it shows there is progress with mindfulness, but it is not about getting somewhere. It is about shedding, about letting go of all that causes us to suffer. It is about discovering where we are and being present in our own lives.

Of course, this is not the only way of setting the scene for the journey of mindfulness, but I have found it very effective. Students seem to find it encouraging, thought-provoking and intriguing.

4 ALLOWING SILENCE TO BE THE TEACHER

"Silence is an empty space, and space is the home of the awakened mind."

The Buddha

When listening to recorded guided meditations I am astounded by just how much most teachers say. Even very experienced teachers say far too much. My sense is that we have got into a cultural mindset that more is better. Well, it isn't. It is a real shame if the opportunity we have when guiding meditations is taken up by the guide not knowing when to keep quiet. As a culture we are very uncomfortable with silence. If there is a gap, our approach tends to be to fill it up.

Remember that guiding a meditation is not about you, it is about your students. It should provide them with an opportunity to become aware of themselves and to see how their own minds function. Now if we talk all the way through the session we are actually doing the meditation for them. It is like going to the gym and getting somebody else to lift the weights and run on the running machine for us.

It serves no purpose if I keep rattling on. In fact, it gets in the way of the students' learning experience. It denies them the opportunity to think and feel for themselves. When a teacher talks too much it may be that they are uncomfortable with silence themselves, or that they want to give their students a pleasant experience so it reflects well on them, or they may just like the sound of their own voice and if they can hear it they feel they are doing a good job. We have to be more courageous. We have to be willing to challenge our students more than we do. There are times when the most effective response to a student is silence. Silence allows students to sense and feel truths for themselves.

Silence and pauses are to me what makes sharing mindfulness magical, and they are so underused, so neglected in our way of life.

Silence

It is no accident that all the major religions have some form of silence in their practice. We cannot listen to God if we are not silent, we cannot appreciate nature if we have a headful of opinions, and we cannot listen to our own wisdom if we are more concerned with listening to our judgments and ideas.

When we bring periods of silence into our classes and indeed into our lives it gives each and every one of us the opportunity to learn, to know something in a different way. Through silence we get a sense of something, we apprehend something without being able to explain it clearly. Silence allows the teachings to have an impact, and our students to be challenged in a way that may be quite new to them.

It does seem though that it is the context within which silence happens that is important. For example, we can be silent all day at home but just keep ourselves very busy, which is not the silence I am talking about. I am talking about an intended silence, a silence which invites us into awareness of the moment, as in meditation or on a meditation retreat or a course, or some other form of spiritual practice. It is not just the absence of sound; in fact it isn't necessarily the absence of sound at all, but a space which we create for listening to the whisper of wisdom.

Silence allows us to process things emotionally and creatively. When we allow ourselves to be silent, we give space for our body to process emotions which often get trapped with over-thinking and busyness. We may also begin to see solutions to problems and issues in our lives which we would not see if we just kept thinking about them.

Silence also allows us to see life more clearly. Often, we see life through our own ideas, our own fears and desires, our own judgments, but when we fall silent even for a short period we get the opportunity to see all these for what they are, impermanent and fluid. Silence can assist us in developing a true insight into our nature and our lives.

At the very beginning of a course, after people have been welcomed at the door and directed to their seats and once everybody is here, we begin - with nothing, or we could say we begin with silence. I will just sit, and everybody else will just sit. If people have been chatting, they sense a shift in the room and often fall quiet.

A few people will look around and I can see them wondering what is going on. They may be wondering if I am okay, or maybe a bit bonkers. After all, they have come to learn mindfulness, so they want to be told what it is. After around two or three minutes I will speak, and ask for responses to that period of silence. Some say they found it calming, others awkward, others say they could not stop thinking. Well, I say to them, we have already started the course. Those moments of silence enabled them to be aware of their experience and that is what we are here to do, to become more aware of ourselves and the world around us.

Later in the course, I will go into a conceptual explanation of what mindfulness is with these students. But I think it is important for them to have a direct taste of mindfulness from the first moment. Beginning the session with a silence sets the tone and the practice for the whole course.

Pauses

Pauses along with silence are what make a mindfulness session not only simple but elegant too.

Pauses are not just something we stick in every now and then when we feel like it; they are an integral part of the session. Put another way, I arrange the material around the pauses. The pauses are as important as the material we teach, the concepts, the metaphors and stories.

Just as salt brings out the taste of other ingredients, so pauses bring out the deeper meaning of a teaching. For example, let's suppose I have just spoken for a few minutes about some aspect of practice or responded to a meaningful question. When I stop speaking it can be a rich time just to pause. This allows what has been said to land, to disturb the student.

Let me use another metaphor. When we give a teaching, it is like throwing a pebble into a pond. After the pebble disappears it disturbs the water bed and slightly clouds the water for a little while. At that moment it is no good throwing another pebble into the pond, then another and another. You will just have a cloudy pond.

This is similar to giving a teaching. It will disturb or challenge the way the student sees themselves or life, so we need to wait a while before launching the next one. We pause and allow what has been said to be digested. This pause, this period of silence, need be only twenty or thirty seconds; it doesn't have to be ten minutes, which would be ridiculous unless it was a meditation. But in those twenty to thirty seconds there is processing going on. We all have filters with which we keep out anything we don't like, and the pause allows the teaching to pass through those filters. These moments are so rich and thrilling. Please don't deprive your students of them.

Un-minding

We can see meditation as a process of what I call un-minding. All day long we are what we could call minding. We are in the mind, thinking about this, that and the other. All this thinking can leave us feeling confused, tense and exhausted.

Of course not all thinking does this, as there is useful thinking, creative thinking and reflective thinking. But most of our thinking is actually unconscious drivel that passes through the mind commenting on everything we do and everything we see.

When we are in the mind, minding, it can create a lot of stress and agitation. So, we each need periods of what I call un-minding. Un-minding is where we simply rest our attention onto one of the senses: let us say sounds, or the feeling of the breeze on the skin, or of course it can be the breath. This un-minding allows un-winding to take place, and gives us the opportunity to see what is going on in our lives.

We can see pausing when teaching as a period of un-minding. When we have given a teaching or responded to a student, we have a pause, a period where we come out of our minds and just relax. This not only helps with what I said earlier about allowing the teaching to land, but it also gives us as teachers an opportunity to sense where to go next. We just sit without thinking much at all, and a new idea, or a new way of expressing something, has the space to pop right up.

When you go to a gallery, the pictures and images are not all scrunched up together. Each painting has space around it, so it can be appreciated. Just so, each of our teachings is a work of art, so treat it that way, and allow your students to appreciate what you are offering them. In my opinion, pausing in this way makes what we do more elegant, and allows our teaching to flow more naturally.

5   WATCHING THOUGHTS

"You have so many views and opinions, what's good and bad, right and wrong, about how things should be. You cling to your views and suffer so much. They are only views, you know."

Ajahn Chah

Thoughts get a lot of attention on mindfulness courses because we all know how much distress they can create. There is a saying in Zen Buddhism: *"The difference between heaven and hell is less than a hair's breadth, and that hair's breadth is the difference between believing a thought and not believing a thought."*

On our courses I always talk quite a lot about thoughts and our relationship to them. This is an area a teacher needs to be clear about, because lack of clarity on the teacher's part can lead to confusion for the students and even make life more difficult for them. There is a risk of students coming to believe that thinking is bad, and that they shouldn't be doing it. If they start to assume that they should be free from thoughts, they could end up giving themselves an unnecessarily hard time.

The teacher's message needs to reassure the student that thoughts are natural. For the sake of simplicity, we can say that there are two types of thoughts, helpful and unhelpful. What many students want, of course, is to stop the unhelpful thoughts - now. However, as teachers we need to teach from our own experience here and show our students how to approach this difficult and often painful experience. We cannot just stop thinking. Instead, we need to show students how to stop feeding the whole momentum of unhelpful thoughts so that they decrease and weaken in intensity quite naturally, just like anything does if it is not nourished and fed.

We all have busy minds, and there are many reasons for this. For a start, most of us are just doing too much. We have too many plans, too many goals, too many responsibilities, too much work. The mind spins trying to keep up, because we don't want it all to fall apart. Let us be clear, there is no quick fix to this busy mind of ours. It is a result of decades of neglecting this area of our experience. Mindfulness can give us some much-needed perspective on this problem of the chattering mind, and some strategies for calming it. We can also come to see that making some small changes in our daily lives, such as learning to pause and be still several times a day, can have a beneficial effect on the state of our minds.

During our teaching of mindfulness we are showing our students that although over-thinking can be painful, the problem does not lie in the thoughts themselves, but rather in our attitude towards them and our relationship with them.

The clicky pen

To help our students understand the nature of thoughts and our relationship to them I pick up a clicky-ended pen, or pretend that I have one. You know what I mean - a ball-point pen where the nib disappears into the pen when you click the other end. Then I say something along the following lines.

See this pen, this pen is a tool. It is a wonderful tool, perfect for writing. It can also be useful for poking holes in plastic bags when you can't open them, but really it is best used for writing, which is what it was made to do.

When you have finished writing a letter with it, what do you do? You click it, the nib goes in, and you put it down to rest until you need it again. This is using it as it was meant to be used, as a tool which is good for a particular purpose.

Now suppose you have finished writing the letter and you click the end, but the nib won't go in and you find the pen won't stop writing. It just carries on writing a load of rubbish. No matter how much you want it to stop writing, it won't. Even when you want to go to sleep this pen carries on writing. This continues day after day after day. It begins to be exhausting.

The thinking mind is like the pen. It is an excellent tool, one we could not live without. It is excellent for working some things out, for planning and analysing and for solving some problems. It is a miracle of nature. But we don't know how to use it. We have lost the art of using the tool of the thinking mind for the purpose it was intended for. We don't need the thinking mind when we are walking down the street, having a shower, appreciating a tree or the ocean. We don't need it to enjoy a cup of tea, or to go to sleep. We have come to over-rely on this one magnificent tool to try to solve all our problems. Think, think, think, - that's what we are now wired to do.

Becoming aware of thinking

As we practice mindfulness over the years, and we come to loosen our attachment to thoughts just a little, we realise that we can of course use the mind but use it more wisely. We can use it when we need it. We don't let it chatter away all day long with judgments and opinions that we are better off without.

When this process begins to happen, we then begin to become aware of other attributes that we possess - the felt sense, the intuition, and our own deeper wisdom that have all been drowned out by the noisy chatter of the over-thinking mind.

Now please don't get me wrong - it is not that the mind never gets out of hand, never thinks when it is not needed. But the sting goes out of it. It loses its power to fool you into thinking that everything it says is meaningful and wise. A beautiful quietness begins to enter into your life.

What we really need to do is to use our own intuitive awareness to see into the nature of thoughts, to see that they are fleeting and insubstantial. Until we really grasp this, all the techniques, all the wishing they would just go away, all the trying to stop thinking just makes it all worse. We need to use awareness, we need to use our own ability to pay attention, to see what the thinking mind is really capable of.

Labelling thoughts

Please try this yourself a few times and then share it with your students or clients. I find this works for everybody, if they are willing to give it a go.

Think of a negative thought that you could have in real life. It may be a criticism of yourself or somebody else. It may be a fear of something happening. For example, it may be something like: "I am so useless, my life is a mess", or "she really hates me, I know she does", or "he always says that, he is such an idiot". Don't pretend you don't have thoughts like this. **Make the thought negative as these are what are problematic for us.**

Repeat it to yourself for twenty seconds. Do that now. OK, so you will see that even under these artificial conditions, thinking those thoughts is unpleasant. Even though we know it is an exercise they still have an impact. Believing thoughts can affect our mood and create strong emotions. This is the power of thoughts when we take them as being facts.

Now I want you to think the same thought again, but this time I want you to say before it the words: "I am having a thought". You say the same thought as before, but just put "I am having a thought" in front of it. For example: "I am having a thought - my life is a mess", or "I am having a thought - he hates me". Do this now for twenty seconds.

I think you will have noticed quite a difference. Putting "I am having a thought" before the thought gives you perspective, distances you from the thought. It allows you to see that it was just a thought and not a fact. I urge you to use the tool of thought labelling whenever you get lost in emotional thinking.

When you have labelled the thought, return back to the body. **If it helps, put your focus on the breath and feel it as it goes in and out. Or count your in-breaths and when you reach ten, start again.** If possible you can come back to the sensation in the body related to the negative thinking, maybe a feeling of heaviness, or anxious tension in the belly or chest. You can make that sensation the object of your awareness. Notice where you feel it, the shape and texture. You will then notice at some point that you have drifted off again into thinking, because this is our habit. So once again, label the thought to remind yourself that it is a thought and not a fact; what I mean is that the story in your head is just a story, it is not really happening. Then return again to what is real - the sensations in the body. These are really happening here and now, so that is where we place our attention.

Please don't give yourself a hard time for having these thoughts, or for drifting off into them over and over again. It is completely normal and inevitable that this should happen. The essential thing is to come to understand that thoughts are unreal; they are just thoughts, nothing more. And this is what labelling helps us to do. If we don't begin to see into the nature of thoughts we will forever be seduced by what they seem to offer us, and unable to detach ourselves from their control.

The fuel and the fire

One metaphor I use around this issue is what I call the fuel and the fire.

Let us suppose for a moment that our emotions are like a fire, and our thoughts are like fuel, or more accurately our believed thoughts are like fuel. It is fuel that keeps a fire burning. Now how do we put out a fire? If we don't have water or anything else to throw over it, we put it out by starving it of fuel. Nothing can exist without fuel, without nourishment.

For example, if we are angry, and we stay in the storyline in our head, going over it again and again, this is pouring fuel on the fire. Our believed thoughts just keep on fuelling the anger. In the Buddhist tradition this is called *upadana,* which can be translated as "clinging". When we cling to the storyline in our head this only serves one purpose, to keep us stuck in that storyline.

All the while we are lost in our heads, trapped in our story lines, the emotions generated by those stories just carry on increasing and intensifying, whether they are anger, anxiety, jealousy, self-pity or whatever. Thought labelling is an excellent way to deal with this, because it allows us to see that a thought is a thought, and not the truth. When we label a thought as a thought we are able to detach from it and gain some much-needed perspective. It is like cleaning dirty windows: suddenly we can see with clarity. However, we will surely find ourselves lost in thinking pretty soon, so we label again and return to the body and the breath - something that is real and tangible.

We need to keep stepping off the merry-go-round of over-thinking in this way to allow ourselves to become familiar and comfortable with our real present-moment experience.

The thought buses

This is a well-known metaphor that I use to give students another strategy for getting perspective on their thoughts or gaining some insight into them.

Imagine you are at the bus stop waiting for the number 12 to take you to X and the number 6 comes along heading for Y, and you jump on it anyway. After a while you realise you are on the wrong bus, jump off and stand at the bus stop again. Then along comes the number 15, you jump on again and this time you realise you are on the way to Z – miles out of your way. Once again you jump off and wait at the bus stop. Can you imagine this happening all day long, all week long, all life long?

Well, that is what can happen with many of us, inside our heads. Along comes a thought bus and off we go. We don't care where it may be taking us; we jump on regardless. Often these thought buses take us for a long eventful ride. If we're lucky it might be fun, but sometimes they can take us to places we definitely don't want to go, places that are very dark, scary and stressful.

If, however, we are able to remain peacefully at the bus stop of the present moment, we will not end up in these anxious places. Through practising mindfulness over time we are able to do just this. When a thought bus comes we can notice, let it pass by or decide that it is useful and consciously get on it.

We will, however, still find ourselves getting on useless thought buses time and again - that is inevitable. But what mindfulness enables us to do is to notice when we are on a thought bus journey, step off the bus without drama, and rest once again at the bus stop.

The art of this particular aspect of mindfulness is just noticing we are on a thought bus and deciding to hop off it. The point is not to criticise ourselves, not to judge ourselves as useless - that is another thought bus - but simply to notice where the bus was heading, get off it and come back to the body and the breath.

6 GUIDING MEDITATIONS

"Meditation should not be regarded as a learning process. It should be regarded as an experiencing process. You should not try to learn from meditation but try to feel it."
Chogyam Trungpa

As teachers guiding meditations, we are not there to give our students an experience. We are there to facilitate their becoming aware of their own experience. We need to be honest about ourselves. Do we want to give them a nice time? Do we want them to say nice things to us after the meditation? These are questions we need to ask ourselves. We are there for them, not for ourselves. Paradoxically, this for me is where the pure joy and satisfaction lies in teaching mindfulness.

When guiding a meditation, we can make it easier on ourselves by not trying to be too clever. My observation through training people is that we try to be original, we try to give a meditation that has not been given before. It is simpler than that. I do realise that it is understandable to do this at first, but through practice and encouragement we can acquire the confidence to approach our teaching with simplicity.

Really, all we need to do is to drop in a few pointers. Don't complicate it. We should remember that meditation is about awareness, not lots of information. Even on the first week of a course I will not say a lot during the meditation. I give some teaching beforehand, then during the meditation I will drop in a few pointers to guide the students in how to observe their own minds and feel their bodies.

Introducing a meditation

If it is the first session, I tend to start with a little on posture. I show people how to sit in meditation using a chair, cushions or a stool. I emphasise being mentally alert and physically relaxed. I suggest people meditate sitting up unless they have a medical issue such as a bad back. I am not fixed on this and it can be a point of contention even among teachers in our organisation. I come from the Buddhist tradition where we don't lie down; if we had tried to, we would have been asked to leave the meditation hall, or at least to sit up and pay attention. Mindfulness meditation is about waking up, and I suggest we adopt whatever posture helps with this. It is not really about what we prefer, but what in the long term will help us become more aware.

I tend to give a short teaching on meditation before I guide a practice. I will emphasise that there is nothing to achieve and that we are not trying to change anything. I will say that we are definitely not trying to get rid of thoughts and to have a blank mind. I don't want to overload them with instruction. The last thing I mention is thought labelling. I ask them simply to notice when they are lost in thoughts and to label it as "thinking" or "I am having a thought", and then to return their attention to the body and the breath - very simple. I don't mention too much as there is plenty of time to get the message across in the enquiry, and also during the other sessions we will have together.

After a few moments we can direct their attention onto their contact with the chair or the floor. After a few more quiet moments we can ask them to sense their hands resting gently together, or on their lap. After a pause we can suggest that they sense their mood. The order of these suggestions doesn't really matter. I think it is too easy to get caught up with a particular sequence and "doing it right". What matters here is awareness, of our experience and what takes us away from our experience. The object of awareness is less important. In other words, the fact that we can be aware is primary, what we are aware of is secondary.

At this point I tend to remain silent for a minute or two just to let the students settle into their own experience, before guiding again.

The Mindfulness of Breathing meditation

I tend to start the course with the Mindfulness of Breathing meditation. This is generally the first meditation we teach as it gives people something to rest their focus on, and this makes it a little easier for beginners to get started with meditation. I do always include the body in this practice, as well as the breath.

What is important is that we are introducing people to feeling the body and the breath, and noticing their thoughts.

After introducing the meditation as outlined in the previous section and spending a few minutes connecting with the body, I then ask students to take their attention to the movement of the body as it breathes, and to feel that movement. I tell them what to look for: is it smooth, is it long and low in the belly or does it feel shallow high in the chest? Then we pause to allow them to follow the pointer. Time and again I hear instructions such as "Feel around the jaw" immediately followed by another instruction. If we give an instruction, we should give space for that to be followed. It is so simple really.

I will leave pauses of thirty seconds or more between instructions to give people time to follow them. I keep the instructions very simple as I don't want to encourage thinking - there will be enough of that going on anyway. I may say things such as: just feel the breath, observe if it feels long and smooth or a little pinched and shallow. I may ask them to notice where their attention wanders to and then label it as "I am having a thought". I will mention sounds and suggest they should allow these to be a part of their present-moment experience.

If at this point we as teachers feel uncomfortable, well, that is our practice: we need to know how to work with feeling uncomfortable. We can, for example, pause and silently acknowledge to ourselves the urge to say more. However, when the time feels right, and that time will be different for each of us, we drop in another pointer.

My next pointer is usually something like: when you find yourself lost in thinking just repeat quietly to yourself "I am having a thought". It is simply a statement to ourselves of what is happening.

In the first couple of weeks of the course I keep the meditations to around ten minutes, building to fifteen or twenty minutes as the course continues. Even early in the course I intentionally leave space without any guidance at all. This is often one of the most difficult elements for new teachers. There are two reasons why I do this. Firstly, from the start I want the students to begin to see where their attention wanders and what the experience of that is like. I want them to get to know their own thinking patterns, and a teacher cannot do that for them. Secondly, I am not trying to give the students an experience.

I think there is an assumption that we need to say a lot to make sure our students have a pleasant time. We may be afraid that if they don't like the meditation it reflects badly on ourselves as the teacher. As teachers we need to move beyond feeling responsible for our students' experience and to do what is best for them in the long term, which may mean that they don't necessarily get pleasure from their meditation in the short term.

Ending a meditation

One of the areas I get asked about a lot is how to bring a meditation to an end. Some teachers ask students to "come back to the room". I don't like this because it presupposes that they are not in the room during the meditation, and mindfulness is about present-moment awareness. Others will ask students to open their eyes gently.

A meditation doesn't need to have a dramatic ending, and I tend to keep it very simple. In the earliest sessions on a course, I may say something like: "In a few moments I will ring the bell to bring this meditation to a close. Once you cease to hear the bell then open your eyes if they are closed, and sit as you wish. Or if you are lying down, take a minute or two then sit as you wish." After a couple of sessions, I move to just quietly saying that in a few moments we will bring the session to a close; then after a slight pause I ring the bell. After a few sessions, when the students are accustomed to our procedure, I drop the verbal input and just ring the bell.

After ringing the bell, I wait a couple of minutes to give people time to do what they need to do. Some will need to stretch, or change their position somehow. I like to wait until they settle back into their new positions and then become still again. This pause also gives them a few moments to absorb what has just been happening in the meditation.

I then move into the enquiry process by asking if anybody has any questions, observations or comments.

The Being at Home meditation

The Being at Home meditation is also known as the Body Scan. It is the second meditation we teach our students. We introduce it through the metaphor of the home we live in.

Introducing the meditation

Most people have a home, at least everybody here has one. Ideally, a home is a place of comfort and pleasure, a place where you can relax and feel safe. Not always of course, but ideally a home is a safe place.

We all have to leave home to go to the shops, go to work, visit family or walk the dog. Gaynor and I like to go to Italy, so we might leave our home for a week or two. When we come back from one of these longer breaks, we check around the house. Any leaky roof tiles? Any sign of a break-in? We look around to see if everything is OK. As we spend time in the house, we like to pay attention to it and care for it. We look after it and it looks after us.

However, we all have another home, and even if we are unfortunate enough not to have a house-home, we have this home. At this point I ask the group what this home might be. Some look at me as if I am an idiot, some say the heart, some say the present moment, and some say the mind or the body. All are correct to some degree, but for the purpose of this meditation, which is to be present in the body, we call the body our home.

We all spend time in our physical home with our families and friends, but how often are we at home here in the body? And how much do we care for it? Our mindfulness practice is learning to be at home in the body, and to care for it in the same way as we care for our house-home. At least if our house-home falls apart we can get another, but we can't do that with our real home, the home which is our body.

If we are honest, we are rarely home. We are more interested in being anywhere but at home in our body in the present-moment. We are not very good at listening to our body's creaky floorboards, or sensing when things are not right. To sense in this way, we need to be present and alive to the body, we need to live in it. So our practice is one of learning to come out of our heads and into our bodies.

Either just before or during the Being at Home meditation I will often explain how to pay attention. I will ask people to think about their right foot: to think about the toes, the toe nails, the shape of the foot and so on. I then ask them to discard this way of paying attention as it is not what we want. Thinking about our foot is not an experience of the foot. I then ask them to imagine or visualise their foot: to picture the shape, the wrinkles, the colour of it and so on. I then ask them to discard this way of paying attention too. Having an image of the foot is not an experience of the foot. I then ask them to have a feeling sense of the foot. When we have a sensation of the foot, we don't have the experience of ten toes and of toe nails, or of the foot's colour or even its shape. When we try to feel the foot in this way, all we really experience is an amorphous mass of tingling energy.

The meditation

In the Being at Home meditation I will invite people to take up their posture as in the Mindfulness of Breathing, which means I don't cover posture in quite the same level of detail here as it has already been done in the first session of the course.

I will be silent for a minute or two, then begin by guiding people onto different parts of the body such as the toes, ankles, hips and so on. I tend not to go through the body systematically, as I don't think it is necessary, although I don't think it is a problem if it is done that way either. I ask people to notice not just how the body feels but how they feel towards the different parts. For example, they may contract whilst feeling into the belly, or be resistant to sensing around the face. We all have different parts of the body that we like and don't like, and it is good to know that for ourselves.

We want our students to notice for themselves just how much they are away from home (their body) and what takes them away. But also, we want them to see what happens to their body when they are lost in anxious or worrying thoughts: it tenses up. We want them also to observe what happens when they return back home to the body or the five senses: it relaxes.

At some point during a Being at Home meditation I will mention sounds. I suggest that if sounds happen, they should allow these sounds to be a part of their present-moment experience, similar to a sensation in the body. I will also remind them about thought labelling during the session.

The Compassion meditation

The Compassion meditation is also known as the Loving-Kindness meditation. It is one of the central meditations in mindfulness, and the focus of Week 7 in our eight-week course. This is how I might approach and guide the simplest form of the Compassion meditation.

Take up your meditation posture and feel your breath for a few minutes. When you feel ready, take your attention to your heart area (middle of the chest) and notice how it feels there. Be honest. Whether you find sadness, happiness, a heavy kind of feeling or virtually nothing, acknowledge it and gently stay with it.

Be interested in what is here right now - but there is no need to judge anything at all. The head judges, not the heart, so just sense into it.

While staying in your heart area, drop in this phrase silently: may I be happy, may I be well. Like a pebble into a pond. Notice any responses you have to these words. Just as in other meditation practices, if you find yourself drifting, then gently and kindly bring yourself back to the present and go back to your heart area.

Nothing needs to happen here. We are not looking for big explosive feelings of empathy. Just plant the seed.

Again drop in a phrase: may my life go well for me . . . may I be healthy and well.

Now take your attention into your breath for a few moments. Relax. Just breathe.

Now bring to mind a good friend - the first person who appears. Have a sense of them and your response to them.

This friend wants to be happy. So let's wish them well. Drop in the phrase silently: may you be happy, may you be well. If you get distracted by thoughts, just return back to your body and a sense of your friend.

Sense into your chest and heart area. Drop in a phrase silently: may your life go well for you. Relax - we are not trying to have an experience.

Drop in the phrase: may you be happy and healthy.

Now let the friend fade from mind and feel your breath. Relax.

Now bring to mind a neutral person - perhaps a checkout person, post person or colleague in another office. Somebody you don't have an intimate connection with.

Just ponder for a few moments: this person wants to be happy, just like me. They have fears and hopes just as I do. Sense this person's life as best you can.

Now drop in the phrases: may you be well, may you be happy.

Drop in another: may you be healthy and happy . . . may your life go well for you.

Stay in your heart area . . . We are just wishing them well.

So now allow all three people to come to mind - yourself, a good friend and a neutral person. Drop in the phrase: may we all be well and happy.

Now before we end, just have a sense of all the people in your life - just a sense, that is all you need. The people you like and people you don't like and people you hardly know. And just drop in the phrase: may we all be well and happy.

Then when you are ready you can open your eyes and sit as you wish.

A meditation on vulnerability

I often use stories or extended metaphors to introduce a meditation. Here is an example of using a story about a cracked vase to approach a meditation on vulnerability, which I might guide later in the course.

A crack in it

The Buddhist master sat and surveyed his students.

One of them then stood up, bowed, then asked him a question. "Please master, can you tell us how we should view our life?"

He sat quietly for a few moments, then reached for a beautiful vase on the table next to him. "See this vase?" he said. "It has a crack in it."

Nobody could see the crack, but he insisted it was there. They were confused.

He said, "Someday this vase will break, it will fall apart. That is the crack in it. So we have to be mindful when holding it. We have to treat it with care. If it were a plastic vase you wouldn't care for it in the same way because it wouldn't break so easily.

"Likewise, we have a crack in us. It is called our future death. Our relationships also have a crack in them, because at some point our loved ones will leave us or we will leave them. That is why our relationships are precious. We need to cherish ourselves and each other, because just like the vase we are precious and easily broken."

Commentary and teaching

There are many cracks in our lives. The wonderful poet and singer-songwriter Leonard Cohen once said: "Everything has a crack in it, it is where the light gets in."

We should look for these cracks as they are our portal to the land of happiness. When we feel vulnerable, this is a crack. Our usual sense of our solid self is being shaken. This anxious quiver should be welcomed and felt in the body. However, for most of the time most of us do what we can to avoid it. What a shame!

These anxious quivers can happen when we have been criticised. Being criticised means our sense of who we are is being challenged. If we can turn toward these moments of vulnerability or the ending of things, then we begin to sense something new. Our sense of ourselves begins to become more fluid, more flexible.

This turning towards the feeling of vulnerability begins to bring us into an intimate relationship with ourselves and the whole of life. We begin to intuitively see that each moment of our life is precious, because it is all we have. There is nothing outside of this moment, except our thoughts that there is something better in some other time and place.

Our mindfulness practice helps us to see this for ourselves, not just as an idea but as a living reality. We begin to understand what the master was saying - that every event, every relationship, every moment has a crack in it and because of this crack it is precious.

After this teaching, I then guide the following meditation or a similar one.

The meditation

Take your seat in meditation. Feel the contact with the chair or cushions. Sense your hands resting in your lap. After a few minutes begin to feel your breath. Really feel it. Now pay particular attention to the beginning of the in-breath and the end of the out-breath.

Allow yourself to feel emotionally what it means to breathe. In this breath is reflected the whole of life, that everything has a beginning and an end. Allow yourself to feel this. Now pay particular attention to the end of the out-breath. Notice what it feels like to let go of this breath. Is there a little holding on, any emotional holding of the breath as it comes to an end?

Spend a few minutes in this space and allow any resistance or fears to be felt.

Now release your awareness of the breath, and reflect that just as the breath has a beginning and an end, so do all your relationships. This is not about becoming depressed but about learning to cherish each other.

Welcome any feelings of sadness, or joy, or whatever arises. Just turn towards these feelings and embrace them. If it gets too much, then stop and give yourself a break. This is a way of learning to become comfortable with vulnerability and to view each moment as precious.

The Just Sitting meditation

This meditation is from the Zoto Zen tradition and is sometimes called Serene Reflection. It is also known as Choiceless Awareness, and is occasionally referred to as a non-meditation, because during it there is no focus and no aim whatsoever – whatever happens, happens. Some people find this liberating, others very difficult because they want something to focus on. I tend to introduce students to it towards the end of the course, and we provide a guide to practising it in the *Awakening Heart* online programme.

We ask students to take up their meditation posture and to feel relaxed and comfortable in it. After a pause for them to settle into the meditation space, we remind them that the practice is simply to notice, to observe whatever arises in awareness.

We may notice a feeling of pressure in our contact with the chair or cushion. We are aware of those sensations for a while, then perhaps we hear a sound, and we just allow ourselves to hear the sound. If thoughts appear in our heads as opinions or judgments, then that is what is arising right now; we notice the thought, recognise it as a thought, and let it go.

We may have a thought such as "I don't know if I am doing this right". Well, it is the belief in the thought that can be problematic, not the thought itself. If that thought appears in our space of awareness, we can just notice that we are having it and then let it disappear. It's possible that we may notice an absence of thoughts, and we can experience that simply for what it is. We may think "I like this", and we can register this and watch that thought as it disappears.

In this meditation we don't intentionally try to do anything. The breath may be observed and experienced for a few moments, and then our attention will be grabbed by something else. It is simply what is happening. There is no right and there is no wrong. In the context of Just Sitting, right and wrong are only thoughts or opinions, which we can observe as they come and go. We may begin to feel tense, or we may begin to feel relaxed; we simply allow ourselves to be that. No struggle. If we find ourselves struggling with something, we simply notice that. We are nobody, going nowhere.

As we practice this meditation over time, we may begin to realise that whatever arises passes away and is not who we are. We come to see that we are not our thoughts, because in the space between two thoughts we don't disappear; in fact, we may feel more alive than ever. We may realise that our feelings change, that sensations and emotions are constantly changing and that everything is in flux. We can realise that the contents of awareness are constantly shifting and are transient, but we don't come to an end. At some point it dawns on us that there is something that does remain – awareness itself.

The space in a room is never affected by the contents of that room. The space doesn't have preferences, it doesn't judge the contents. If you throw a pot of paint into the air, space is not affected by it. Awareness is analogous to space. In the metaphor of the contents and the container, it is unaffected by the contents but allows all to be.

Just Sitting is such a simple practice, but it can reveal a lot to us about who we are.

Guiding other meditations

The Mindfulness of Breathing meditation and the Being at Home meditation are the first ones we guide our students through at Be Mindful CIC, and they are fundamental to mindfulness practice. We return to them repeatedly during the eight-week course. As the course progresses we also introduce and practise other meditations, most notably the Compassion meditation, the Dancing with Dragons or Untying Emotional Knots meditation, and the Just Sitting meditation.

For teachers, the underlying principles for guiding students through all meditations remain the same. In all cases, we are encouraging our students to become aware of their present-moment experience and to feel how their body responds to it. The various approaches outlined in this chapter are transferable to other meditations practised within our courses at Be Mindful CIC, and also in Mindfulness-Based Stress Reduction and Mindfulness-Based Cognitive Therapy courses.

7   ENQUIRY: TRUSTING SIMPLICITY

"Meditation practice isn't about trying to throw ourselves away and become something better, it's about befriending who we are."

Pema Chodron

Enquiry is the mutual exploration of both the student's and the group's present-moment experience and, just as importantly, their interpretation of and response to their experience. The teacher's role is to facilitate that. This requires the skill of holding the space, sometimes in silence, for students to realise what is happening.

I don't find it easy to write about enquiry, as it is a very personal and in-the-moment experience. Different styles of leading enquiry suit different people, and I don't think any one style is better than any other. It is part of my own character to move away from working within a structure to sensing how things are going and where they need to go, so I lean towards an open style of enquiry. I often use a shrug of the shoulders, a smile, raised eyebrows and silence, to encourage students to explore further. Or, if I feel that an intervention might be useful to move the discussion on, I might throw out a question to the whole group. It is very much a case of responding to the feeling in the room, moment by moment.

That said, I shall offer a few reflections and suggestions.

The purpose of enquiry

The purpose of enquiry has to be the same as the purpose of mindfulness – to alleviate our suffering and distress.

It might be helpful if I list a few of the main aims of enquiry as I see it, although this list is certainly not exhaustive:

> to try to draw out what the participants noticed during the meditation session and how they responded to what they noticed;
>
> to help students discover something about their experience, particularly their thinking patterns and the accompanying bodily sensations;
>
> to gain insight into what arises - thoughts and bodily sensations - and to realise intuitively that everything arises and passes away;
>
> to encourage students to enquire into their own experience from moment to moment;
>
> to help students see how they habitually relate to their experience;

> to reach the understanding that to be aware is effortless, so there is no point in trying to be mindful;
>
> to move beyond concepts to a more direct experience of life.

My main overall objective during enquiry, however, is always to be showing the students how simple mindfulness is, and how simple life can be when we are not lost in concepts and ideas about it. Each student has a mental picture of how life should be, and post-meditation enquiry offers the teacher the perfect opportunity to reveal again and again how clinging to this picture creates suffering for them. The picture is partly made up of broad attitudes such as: people should like me; pain shouldn't happen; things should go my way; life should be pleasant - and many, many, more. We also have particular ones which reveal themselves in our personal relationships, such as: he should love me; she should care for me more; I should be better at my job by now; I should be kinder; she should show more consideration - and many more. List your own!

Enquiry, then, is an excellent opportunity to show students how they grasp onto their picture of how they assume life should be. Their picture will show up in meditation itself; they may cling to the belief that their mind should be quiet or blank, that they should feel relaxed during the session, that meditation will fix them in some way, that they will not feel anything bad anymore. We can illustrate how clinging to the picture, to these beliefs, is what actually prevents them from relaxing. Meditation is seeing clearly, and not trying endlessly to engineer our experience to fit our imaginary picture. With our encouragement, they can begin to see that mindfulness is noticing that they are clinging to the picture, and gradually becoming able to allow their experience to be just as it is. This is trusting in simplicity, trusting in being aware of our experience and not trying to manipulate it. This is ultimately an act of compassion because it gradually diminishes our self-inflicted suffering caused by clinging.

Preparing for the enquiry

The enquiry begins before the meditation. The effectiveness of the enquiry is related to how the teacher sets up the meditation. I think it is good practice to give some hints on what to look for during meditation. This may be said beforehand, and also gentle reminders may be given occasionally during the meditation itself.

For example, we can bring people's attention to the quality of the breath. We can ask what happens to the body when they are listening to sounds or feeling the breath. We can suggest they notice what happens to the body when they are lost in thinking, or whether they feel any tension or other sensations. We can ask if staying with something in the body leads to that sensation reducing. We can suggest that they observe what happens - to anger for instance, or regret, or stress, or sadness - when we dwell in the story line about it.

Opening the enquiry

At the end of a meditation I may take a few minutes before saying anything. Firstly, this is related to one of the three pillars – elegance. I think it more elegant to give some space between activities rather than cramming stuff in. Secondly, I like the students to absorb what has just happened and to have time to orientate themselves towards the enquiry.

I prefer to open the enquiry with something very general. I might ask if anybody has any observations they would like to make about the meditation, or if there are any questions about it. I prefer not to ask people how they are feeling now. This is because implied in that question are the assumptions that we are trying to change how we feel and that if you meditate you will feel better. In the longer term yes, we do tend to feel better, but we need to encourage our students to take a longer-term view of practice and not expect immediate results.

The real difference we want to bring about is a deeper understanding of feelings, that they arise and pass away, that we don't have to spend our time judging and monitoring them. We learn to let feelings and thoughts be, and let them move through us. We want to show our students that they can unhook from thoughts and allow feelings to be held in awareness. This longer-term view is far healthier than forever trying to change how we feel. It allows us to relax into our present experience even when we don't feel so good.

If there aren't any comments coming back after your initial question, don't feel you have to rush in. Be silent, let the question land, and allow time and space. After a while, if nothing has been said, I may decide to ask another question, such as: did you notice what happened when you were lost in thought? Did you observe how the body was when you heard the church bells? Here, the pointers given before the meditation become useful, as you can pick up on one or two of those.

If there still aren't any questions or comments, I may threaten to ramble on some more. I say this jokingly of course, and it normally raises a few laughs. It also usually breaks the ice and prompts someone into saying something.

Doing the enquiry

During enquiry, students have the opportunity to raise any difficulty they had during the meditation, if they wish to; it offers a way of exploring how they were with that. For the teacher, this may involve asking something like: what did you do at that point? Were you okay with that? Where in the body did you feel that?

Of course, students may also comment positively on aspects of the meditation and their response to it. Enquiry is a space in which individual experiences can be shared, providing fresh insights and perspectives, as well as opening students to challenges experienced by others in the group.

The opportunity might also arise to help students understand how they habitually relate to their experience. For example, when a student experiences sadness, perhaps they might intellectualise it or want to deny it. If this emerges during enquiry, we can suggest that this may be a habitual response, and offer possible alternative approaches for when it happens again. For example, they could try to turn towards the sadness, be curious about where in the body it is felt, and experience what it actually feels like, rather than what they assume it feels like.

If the student seems okay with this, we could ask further questions which point towards different possible ways of relating to their sadness. How did/do you feel towards it? Did you notice your thoughts about it? If so, what happened to your experience at that point? Where did you feel it in the body? How does it feel if you take away the label "sadness"?

At some point we can move away from speaking to that student to making a more general point to the group. This is a good art to master – to know when to move from speaking to a particular student to speaking more generally to everyone in the room. This skill is also useful if you think the student may feel a little uncomfortable with too much spotlight.

A teacher also needs to know when to end an enquiry with a person. You can actually ask them: would you like to say anything else? At other times it may be obvious that they understand, or you can intuit that they don't want to say anything more - in which case silence is appropriate.

During enquiry we are exploring another person's, or several people's, experience of the meditation. We need to be gentle and firm, curious and sensitive, warm and also respectful of their limits. We also need to tune in to body language and read when somebody may have said enough, or if they want to say more but are a bit stuck.

During enquiry you can, as with teaching, draw on stories, parables and poetry as a way of explaining your point. For example, if you are talking about welcoming difficult emotions, the poem "The Guest House" by the thirteenth-century Iranian poet Rumi explains it beautifully. The translation by Coleman Barks is used frequently in mindfulness groups, and is easily to be found on the Internet. The central message of this poem is one of the core messages of mindfulness meditation - to be with whatever life brings to us.

When doing enquiry, I am not really giving answers. I am responding, to the best of my ability, to help the student and the group become more aware of themselves and how they function. It is important to remember that as a teacher you can only aid this process; you are not responsible for it.

8   DANCING WITH DRAGONS

"Meditation can help us embrace our worries, our fear, our anger; and that is very healing. We let our own natural capacity of healing do the work."
Thich Nhat Hanh

What is it we are trying to do when teaching mindfulness? In my view we are showing our students how to become aware of their own experience and the world around them, and through this relieve their dissatisfaction and unhappiness. When the Buddha was asked what he taught, he replied that he taught the end of suffering. If that was good enough for him then it is certainly good enough for me. Of course, there are other by-products of practice, such as better health and greater performance in certain fields, but for me the relief of suffering is the essence.

Dragons are fierce and scary, but also wonderful and mysterious, much like our emotional life. Our meditation is a way of learning to turn towards these dragons and dance with them, rather than trying in vain to rid ourselves of them.

Your secret practice

Most of us who practise meditation have a secret agenda or a secret practice, what one teacher called our hidden practice. Our secret practice is our deeper reason for practising meditation, and it takes honesty to uncover it. It may not be completely secret from ourselves, but because we are rarely totally honest with ourselves it remains in the shadows. For example, we may experience feelings of shame or guilt, and of course we don't like having them. So we take up meditation with the idea that we will somehow cure ourselves of these feelings. We may use all the right language of accepting them, letting them be, and welcoming them, but if we look with honesty, we must acknowledge that we really want to be rid of them.

People on my courses often ask me whether, if they accept these feelings, they will go away. This is exactly the reason they are still present, because this attitude leads only to more internal conflict. There is a part of me which doesn't like some other parts of me and is trying to get rid of those parts.

What we are doing here is taking profound and transformative notions of acceptance, letting be and so on, and trying to turn them into mere techniques with which to cure our problems. So instead of meditation being a healing space, we turn it into our weapon of choice with which to go to war on ourselves. One side of our personality takes up arms against the other side, and of course meditation is a great weapon because it is done with the notion of being spiritual and compassionate. So the hidden war goes on.

Our secret practice is bred by a fantasy - the fantasy that meditation will cure us of anything unpleasant, or that it will make us kinder, more compassionate, wiser, more confident or whatever. Meditation can of course help us to cultivate these qualities, but not if we use it to go to war on ourselves. We cannot expect to be more compassionate when we fight against feelings we don't like. Being compassionate means learning to experience and to feel all those feelings we don't want to feel, and not just the pleasant ones.

A few years ago my father died, my wife's eyesight seemed to be failing and my dog was ill. During that period, I woke up one particular morning feeling deeply sad. I then took myself into my meditation space and sat down. I have made honesty with myself my practice, and I had to admit that I just wanted to feel better. However, instead of playing into that game, I took my attention to the sensations of deep sadness and stayed with them. I became curious about them and just felt them. There was a ring of sorrow in my heart and chest. Tears came and went. After twenty minutes or so I felt the tension easing and the weight lifting. What had happened was that I had stopped fighting against it. All my opinions and judgments - about how bad this was, how I didn't like it, how I wished it would all go away - were absent. I felt lighter. I had allowed myself just to feel the sadness, and really that is all we need to do. This was me learning to dance with the dragon of sadness.

Our meditation practice can so easily become a means of steering away from these uncomfortable areas of our lives, when really we need to be steering towards them. This is why honesty is so crucial in our practice. When you sit in meditation and you are honest about your intention, then the transformation has begun.

The path of mindfulness is the path of honesty with ourselves. Honesty allows us to acknowledge what is really going on in any moment. Honesty and curiosity are the two qualities which help us reveal our secret practice.

Questions are an excellent tool for unearthing our secret practice. I often use questions, and suggest my students use them too. For example, I may ask myself what is going on right now, or I may notice that I feel hurt, sad or uneasy in some way. If I am at work or busy in my daily life, I may have to decide that now is not a good time to have a look at this right now.

Once we acknowledge that we have a secret practice, we know that our students have one too, so we can help them. Of course, our secret practices are not identical, because each of us has different things we like and dislike about ourselves. One student may have unacknowledged anger; another may experience lots of shame; another may find sexuality difficult to acknowledge; another may be very uncomfortable with sadness. However, the healing of this is always to be honest and curious, and to learn how to experience these unwanted parts of ourselves.

Two pools of practice

One of my favourite metaphors is that of the two pools, from the Zen tradition. It perfectly sums up two different approaches to practice.

Imagine there are two pools, Pool A and Pool B. These pools look a little strange because they both have rubbish around the outside.

Person A goes to Pool A, jumps over the rubbish and into the pool, and has a good time. They get out and dry off. They feel refreshed for a while, a few hours. They do this day after day. No matter how many times they enter the pool, it still looks the same, with the rubbish around the outside. In fact the rubbish slowly builds up.

Person B would rather go to Pool B, but there is something different about how this person enters the pool. As they get to the side of the pool they pick up a little of the rubbish and dive in. The pool cleans up the rubbish, so when they get out with it they realise it is no longer rubbish but has transformed into something else. They may or may not feel refreshed, but they are not so concerned with how they feel immediately. The point is that there is now less rubbish around the pool, for the next time they come.

The pools represent two approaches to practice. The Pool A approach is where we just want to ignore our rubbish. We don't want to look at any difficulties, we just want the bliss. This was originally my own approach to practice. The problem with this approach to meditation is that the rubbish keeps building up. In the Pool B approach we are willing to take the rubbish into the pool with us, a little at a time, and so over time it gets cleaned up.

Although Pool A looks like Pool B, they are not the same. The first pool is the approach of concentration, often mistaken for mindfulness. Concentration is of course useful, but it is only one facet of the jewel of mindfulness. A practice based merely on concentration is one where we block out anything which troubles us. In teaching we may tell our students to just come back to the breath if something bothers them. That may help them to feel better in the short term but in the long term it will not get them very far. We need to show them how to take their rubbish into the pool for it to be cleaned up. The way to clean up the rubbish, or a better term would be to transform it, is to experience it in the body.

My question to you is: which pool of practice do you go into each day? And just as importantly: which pool of practice are you teaching your students?

The Dancing with Dragons meditation

I often use the "Two pools of practice" metaphor to introduce this meditation, which is also known as Untying Emotional Knots or Working with Difficulties. It is the central focus of Week 5 on our eight-week course. However, we cannot really help touching on this topic every week, as questions about difficult emotions are always arising.

I usually begin this meditation by asking students to be curious about their present-moment experience in the body and to see if anything needs attention: for example, a tension, a tightness or an uneasiness somewhere. This is the equivalent of picking up a little rubbish to take into the pool with you, and not ignoring it in the pursuit of some abstract blissful state of mind. Or I may ask them to begin the meditation practice with the question: what don't I want to face in myself right now? This is being honest and acknowledging that there are going to be things about myself that I don't want to face.

After asking the question, we have to be willing to be curious about where it is felt in the body and really honest about how it feels and our attitude towards that feeling. We then just sit with it and let it be. We don't do anything towards it. We don't zap it with healing lights and try to change it in any way. We leave it be and hold it in awareness. This is how change happens; it is a natural consequence of experiencing without interference and without wanting to force change to occur.

A good way of adopting this way of practising with difficulties is to actually notice what the physical sensation feels like. Does it feel heavy or light? Does it feel hot or cold? Hard or soft? Does it have a shape? We may also notice how it feels emotionally; we may observe some sadness or anger or another uncomfortable emotion. We may notice that it is related in some way to an event in our life, such as a communication problem or a relationship.

However, we need to just hold it in awareness and not look for results. If we are looking for results then we are not present with it, and again we are into an agenda. If you are truly compassionate to a friend who is in pain, you are not looking for a result or to fix them. The same goes for being with our own pain. We just learn to feel and listen. We are not here to fix ourselves.

It can take a while, months and sometimes years, to begin to turn our attitude from one of wanting benefits to just doing the practice and letting the benefits arise.

Idiot compassion and challenging your students

Most people who walk through the door of the mindfulness room for the first time come for the wrong reason. They come in order to be fixed, to be cured, perhaps even for you to do it for them. They may come with the idea that they need to get rid of some part of themselves or to become a better person.

The Buddhist teacher Chogyam Trungpa coined the phrase "idiot compassion" to describe compassion that is unreal and unhelpful. He defines an idiot as someone who is "senseless", who does not think intelligently. "Idiot compassion" is showing deep heartfelt concern when we do not really feel it. This is often an unthinking, knee-jerk response, which might take the form of saying something like: "Oh you poor thing, how awful that must be!" Chogyam Trungpa describes this as "the compassion of the ego", because it is motivated not by genuine concern for the other person, but by a desire to be liked or to feel good about ourselves.

However, compassion in the true sense is not this wishy-washy "oh how awful that must be" attitude. Compassion in the Buddhist tradition is often depicted as being wrathful and powerful; it is not just depicted as pink lotuses. In our teaching, compassion is doing and saying what is necessary to help a student become clear about what creates their own suffering. To do this we have to use our intelligence, be honest and be willing to challenge. We have to be prepared for the student to feel a little uncomfortable, as this may be the first time somebody has challenged them in this way.

There is a difference between causing pain and causing harm. In my teaching I may occasionally have to cause some pain or at least discomfort, but my intention is not to hurt or harm the students in any way; it is to wake them up. As a consequence I may need to disagree with something one of them has said, in which case I need to be willing to say: "Wait a minute, is that true?"

At other times, I may know somebody is holding an unhelpful view but instead of speaking directly to them I may speak to the group, so it does not hurt quite so much and I don't put an individual on the spot. As teachers we have to read what is in the room. We don't always get it perfectly right, but if our intention is good we won't go far wrong.

We can only challenge, though, if we keep our own sensitivity; otherwise we could be a little brutal and that of course is out of the question. To paraphrase T. S. Eliot, people can't bear too much reality, so we challenge our students, but not too much or too soon. We want to leave them with something to ponder, something to consider about themselves and their lives.

A good challenge may not be something said; it may be just a pause, a few moments of silence. These moments can allow realisations to occur. Something may dawn on the students in those few moments of quiet.

What I have seen is that if you are willing to challenge your students, they come to trust you. They see you are not there just to be liked, but that you have their welfare at heart because you are willing to stick your neck out for them. Invariably towards the end of a course or a retreat they show their appreciation. It may be the first time that somebody has challenged them in that way and it is what they have been waiting for.

This can be one of the most difficult areas for teachers, because we don't want to be seen as mean, or we may be just not very good at disagreeing. So we can easily err on the side of caution and not really challenge at all. I think this is a real shame, as coming along to a mindfulness course is a wonderful opportunity for somebody to transform their life. Teachers are there to help this happen, not to give themselves and the students a nice time.

Working with difficult emotions and pain

Working with difficult emotions can be one of the most challenging aspects of teaching. As teachers we want to be able to work with our own before helping others. We need to be okay with feeling uncomfortable emotionally and to know how to embrace and to work through this process.

We all have unresolved emotions. A lot of our thinking is a protection against feeling these emotions. How often do we feel hurt and just keep on going over the same thing again and again, keeping busy?

I often say on retreats that it is not the emotions we experience that are so problematic, but the ones we don't. These unacknowledged emotions can become lodged in the body, weighing us down and making life feel heavy. Every one of us has to some degree what we can call unacknowledged sadness or anger, which left that way may cause depression or at least this sense of heaviness, which some people carry around with them.

When I first visited Vajraloka Retreat Centre in Wales in the 1990s, one of the teachers said something which changed my practice forever. He said that sometimes we need to go "looking for trouble". Up until that point I had seen meditation as simply a matter of following the breath. My practice until then had been to get away from myself, my troubles and my feelings, in the hope that meditation would somehow cure me.

What the teacher at Vajraloka was saying was that meditation is done with the body, not the mind. We need to be curious about the sensations in the body, because the body carries the unresolved past. He said that we can learn to read the signs in the body. I found this very interesting, so my own practice developed. From then on, when I practised with the breath I would also have a sense of the body and what was happening in it. I would occasionally go and see what I could find, "looking for trouble", and there is often something to be found. It could be a heaviness in the chest, a contraction in the throat, a holding in the belly and more.

What we really need to do is to turn toward the hurt and feel it in the body. We need to notice where it is and observe what it feels like. We need to label our thoughts and keep returning to the sensations in the body, really experiencing the physical effects that we feel. After a time, we will find that the mind begins to calm down.

Of course, for some of us the body is a place of pain, so we don't want to be there with it. However, no matter how painful it feels, it is still our home. The key here is how we relate to the pain. I don't want to sound glib about deep pain, but whether we like it or not we are in relationship to it. Practising mindfulness can change that relationship from one of resistance and loathing to one of acceptance and learning to be more at ease with what we find uncomfortable. That doesn't mean we don't take medication and undergo treatments to alleviate physical pain, but through meditation we can also begin to relate differently to it.

Being honest with ourselves

Read this short section, then try doing it.

Close your eyes. Ask yourself: why do I practice meditation? Don't ask your head, but drop it into your being, as it were.

Wait for a response. There will be one, even if it is a very subtle sensation somewhere in the body, or some subtle thoughts connected with the question. There may be thoughts which distract you from this deep listening. Notice these and return back to the body. People often ask how I know the difference between thoughts which are useful and those which are not. When you listen deeply you will know. There is a felt rightness about the whole experience.

Always return back to the body. Feel those sensations in it. They may be a little uncomfortable, or not.

This is our first response to the question. However, we don't just stop there.

After a minute or two ask yourself: why do I ***really*** practice meditation?

Then notice what else arises. There will be thoughts, and we can acknowledge them, as before, always returning to the body. Again, be aware of any subtle or not-so-subtle responses in the body. These can often be felt around the chest or belly area.

I don't want to say too much about this short practice as that could influence your experience of it. Just give it a try. Really this is about listening to the body and the responses within it.

9   GOING BEYOND CLICHÉS

"The problem with clichés is not that they contain false ideas, but rather that they are superficial articulations of very good ones."

Alain de Botton

Clichés are very common in the mindfulness world. I read recently that mindfulness is nothing but a bunch of tired clichés, constantly reworded slightly to clog up our Instagram and Facebook feeds. I am not surprised by this criticism. It is not that the clichés are necessarily wrong, but that they are overused, or so often used in a lazy and uncritical way.

Let's just name some for starters. Mindfulness students are frequently encouraged to "let go", to "sit with it" or "be with it", to cultivate "acceptance" and to "live in the present moment". They are urged to "be kind to yourself", "have self-compassion" or "be non-judgmental". But are we all sure that we know what these tired old phrases actually mean?

"Live in the present moment" is very easy to say, but does it stand up to scrutiny? If you nearly get run over by a bus, or are lost in wonder at a beautiful sunset, it is possible to be "in the moment" quite naturally for a few seconds, entirely focused on the immediate experience and undistracted by anything else. But then that sense of presence will be broken, some other thought will intrude, and the old chattering mind will be back. It is simply impossible to turn off the mind for more than a few seconds at a time. You cannot just live in the moment all the time through a certain kind of effort. So, if teachers want to use this phrase, they must be very clear about what they mean by it, and convey this meaning to their students.

I am not saying we should not use this term or any of the others I mention, but we need to be able to explore the deeper meaning.

On our teacher training programme, each trainee is given the opportunity to guide meditations and to give a presentation on what mindfulness is. If they use one of those overused words or phrases, we will ask them to explain what they really mean by it. If you have a person in your class who is suffering, perhaps with grief or sadness or something more physical, then asking them to "accept" it is not good enough. We have to get behind the word and explain how to do it. This is the difficult part. We have to illustrate and show them what acceptance really is, not just hit them with the word.

Acceptance

There are two qualities that we need for an effective mindfulness practice: activity (doing) and receptivity (being). They are not separate. They work together or not at all, like the two wings of a bird. A bird with one wing cannot fly.

One definition of acceptance in the Oxford online dictionary is: "the action of consenting to receive or undertake something offered". The key word here is "action". Acceptance is something we do. It is an engagement with what the present moment is offering. For example, let us say I have a sad feeling. What does it mean to accept that?

Firstly, it means being honest enough to admit to myself that I feel sad. Secondly, it means being curious about this feeling of sadness, and exploring where in the body I am feeling it. This may take a little while to discover, but the curiosity takes me out of my thinking mind and into a felt sense of what is going on in the body. This is the active wing of the bird of practice. I am being actively curious. I am curious about where I feel the sadness and also what it feels like. I would ask my students to notice two or three qualities of the sensation of sadness.

I give the sensation of sadness some space to just exist. I welcome it and let it rest in awareness. I don't try to do something to it, I don't try to get rid of it, I don't try to change it into something else. I allow it to unfold, giving it space to be exactly as it needs to be. I am receptive to it. This is the other wing of practice, receptivity. I don't have opinions about it, or if I do, then I just acknowledge those and come back to the felt sense of the sadness. An aspect of receptivity is listening. So in a sense I just listen to it.

In the Buddhist tradition there was a Tibetan teacher called Milarepa who was a real character. There is a wonderful image of Milarepa sitting on a lotus with his hand cupped behind his ear, just listening. This image sums up the path: we need to listen to each moment of our life.

As we give the sad feeling the space to be, it naturally transforms itself. Sadness is the seed of compassion. If we don't allow ourselves to experience the sadness, we cannot experience compassion.

I have focused here on the inner world, but it is similar in the external world too. We need to accept what is in front of our eyes if we are to change what is. Acceptance is a position of power, not resignation.

Let go

"Let go, just let go" is another of those terms that is very easy to say but can be misleading to somebody new to mindfulness.

We cannot let go of what we do not possess, or at least what we do not acknowledge. If someone is feeling sad, resentful or angry it is no good suggesting that they should let go of that feeling. If someone is bringing up the past again and again, saying "let go" is not going to make much of a difference to them. It might even just annoy them.

The problem we humans have is that we cling. This is basic Buddhism, and if you were to become familiar with the roots of mindfulness and explore Buddhism it would only help your teaching. The cause of suffering is *trisna*, a kind of deep thirst which results in clinging.

Clinging or craving is an expression of addiction, and we are all addicted in some way. We are addicted to our thoughts, our hopes, our desires, and especially to having an identity. Even if that identity is of somebody who suffers and feels inferior to other people, we don't really mind; we want to feel we know who we are, and that is far more important to us than being happy.

Letting go of the cravings and addictions that make us unhappy is difficult. It isn't something we can just do out of thin air. We might manage it for a few moments, but that pendulum will swing back again.

Let us suppose that I am ruminating on something somebody did to me months ago. I talk about it a lot. I tell people how bad this person was to me. I am addicted to the resentment I feel towards this person, and clinging to it is making me very unhappy and dissatisfied. If I am to move on from this, I need to be honest with myself about what is going on. I also need to be willing to do something about it.

I could begin by placing my attention on the breath, as in a Mindfulness of Breathing meditation. Then I notice when my attention wanders and where it wanders to. I label that thought and then come back to what is real, my bodily sensations and my senses.

At some point the resentment that I just mentioned will pop up. (Alternatively, I could go looking for it and make it come to the surface.) At that point I label the thought, but instead of going back to the breath I become curious about the emotional aspect of resentment. All those thoughts are the tip of the iceberg and they keep popping up because I have unresolved emotions to do with this person. If we don't resolve the emotional aspect, the thoughts will hover in the background ready to hijack our attention and even disrupt our lives.

So there is truth in the term "let go", but we need also to turn toward the emotion in the body as in the section on acceptance. Once we resolve the emotional aspect, those thoughts will weaken over time. Letting go is a natural outcome of healing.

Is that so?

There was once an old farmer who lived a simple life with his son. One day his horse ran away. Upon hearing the news, his neighbours came to visit.

"Such bad luck," they said, feeling for the farmer.

"Is that so?" the farmer replied.

The next morning the horse returned, bringing with it three other wild horses.

"How wonderful!" the neighbours said.

"Is that so?" replied the old farmer.

The following day, his son tried to ride one of the untamed horses, was thrown off, and broke his leg. The neighbours again came to say how sorry they were.

"Is that so?" answered the farmer.

The day after, military officials came to the village to draft young men into the army. Seeing that the son's leg was broken, they passed him by. The neighbours congratulated the farmer on how well things had turned out.

"Is that so?" replied the farmer.

I love this story, because it exemplifies deep acceptance of the moment and not panicking. True acceptance comes from knowing that everything changes. The farmer let go of any fixed positions; he was able to follow that other much overused cliché, to "go with the flow".

It also points to living in the present moment because he did not let his thoughts of what might be take him to some imagined outcome, but stayed with the uncertainty of life. He didn't get pulled out of the present, or the perspective that we really don't know what will result from actions and events.

Being present doesn't mean there is a certainty to life, but just the opposite. It means being with the absolute uncertainty of what is just around the corner.

Sit with it

You may have been on a mindfulness course or been running one yourself, and you have heard or used the terms "sit with it" or "be with it". They are so very easy to say, but what do they really mean? I hear them often in response to a comment or question around discomfort or difficult emotions. I think, though, that when somebody is struggling with any form of discomfort we need to give them more than suggesting they sit with it. We need to show them *how* to sit with it. The clue is really around curiosity.

Often when somebody has discomfort then what they experience is not the direct experience of the sensations of discomfort, but their beliefs, judgments and thoughts about it. A person's belief may be that this pain is around all the time. Or that this pain is somehow solid and unyielding. Judgments may be thoughts like "I hate this" or "I just want this to go away". Now of course we want to be free from pain, but these thoughts, which we can replay on a loop over and again, do not help in any way.

Many people new to mindfulness, and even some more experienced people, don't know the difference between thoughts and sensations, but knowing this difference is crucial if we are to move into really sitting with something. If we become curious about the qualities of a sensation, then we can come out of our judgments and beliefs about it. We can begin to observe its qualities directly, and not get caught up in our thoughts about it. I often ask people to name three qualities of the sensation. Perhaps through observation they can see if it is heavy or light. I may ask: does it have a shape or colour? Does it have a texture? After a time I may ask if there is an emotion connected with this. Does it feel sad, angry or scared?

Of course, not everybody wants to do this, and permission is always given for somebody to stop when they have done enough. But this is what it means to sit with discomfort; it is not just a "grin and bear it" kind of attitude.

All this does not mean that if we are in physical pain we should not take whatever medication or treatment we can to alleviate our pain. It is also worth saying here that if any discomfort during meditation can be alleviated simply by changing posture then of course we should do that.

Be kind to yourself

Compassion is a key quality that we want to integrate into our life and of course into our teaching. However, Chogyam Trungpa's term "idiot compassion" describes what most of us do a lot and call it compassion; he explains it as being nice. Pema Chodron similarly warns against our tendency to give people what they want because we can't bear to see them suffer.

There is of course a danger in the "idiot compassion" approach. It is as if a friend were taking poison which they think is good for them and instead of offering them medicine which may not taste very nice – as mindfulness often doesn't - we give them more poison because we don't want them to dislike us or be offended. This is more about ourselves and how we feel than about our suffering friend.

In the context of teaching, compassion means being willing to challenge our students. It is so very easy to use the terms such as "whatever works for you" or "be kind to yourself", when in fact what a student may need is to be challenged. I am not saying we should never use these terms, as sometimes they are what needs saying, but we need to be aware of our motive. For example, if a student is saying that they are not meditating then we can ask why, we can challenge them, we can explore that issue. If another student is living in a way that is obviously causing them to suffer, then as teachers we need to have the courage to explore that with them.

If a student is telling me that somebody is being critical of them and causing them distress, I will explore the issue with them. If appropriate, I will move the attention from that student and speak more generally, so they don't feel too much in the spotlight. My aim is to encourage them to see that they are causing themselves to suffer through the very way they think about it. They may have to decide whether to continue to spend time with that person. At these moments I may bring in teachings such as the two arrows and explore it that way.

If somebody wants to lie down during meditation I won't just say "Oh that's fine, do what you need to do"; I will ask them why. Lying down may be appropriate for them at that particular moment because they are tired or have a bad back, or it may be a way of not facing themselves. Just saying "oh that's fine" may be feeding them more poison. Being kind to ourselves doesn't always mean doing what is easiest.

"Be non-judgmental" can be another easy phrase to throw in. It is not that there isn't some truth in it - of course there is. But we all know that judging thoughts just happen, whether we like it or not, and we have to deal with them. What we can do, and what I think is a much healthier way to practise, is to observe those thoughts or to label them. The problem lies in the indulgence of these judging thoughts, not in the arising of them.

*

My suggestion is to reflect on all these much-used terms and to get behind them. What do they really mean? What are they really pointing to? Remember that words are only pointers, they are not the thing itself. The word "moon" is not the moon; it is only pointing to the moon. The words "New York" are not New York; they are only a pointer.

If you are willing to do this, then your teaching will take on a much deeper feel for your students. They will sense that they are in the presence of somebody who knows what they are saying, somebody they can trust to teach them this ancient and wonderful practice.

10   TEACHING INTUITIVELY

"Intuition doesn't tell you what you want to hear; it tells you what you need to hear."

Sonia Choquette

We cannot describe intuition, because it is indescribable. We can try to point to it, but we need to do this intuitively and not analytically. If we approach this with our heads we will try to pin down intuition and want to discover exact information about it, as if it were a butterfly pinned to a board and we were describing in detail its wing span, species, colour, country of origin and so on. That won't get us very far. My dictionary defines intuition as "a kind of sixth sense or a second sight". That is one way of trying to apprehend it. I like to see it as a jewel with many facets. One of these is using our instincts; another is listening to that sense of silent felt knowing; another is understanding something without conscious reasoning. Some people call it gut instinct and others say it's just having an indefinable sense of something. All these ideas are helpful, and point to our intuition.

In this chapter I want to explore intuitive teaching, and how it is not only very useful for our students but can also be a magical experience for the teacher.

Accessing your intuition

Many people ask me how to access intuition. It's not easy to answer that question as intuition is not a thing, it's a kind of knowing. There are two main ways of knowing: the rational and the intuitive. You might know something rationally because it's a fact that you remember or can work out, like 2+2=4. The rational approach is a kind of linear process; it involves consciously using your mind to think something through and reach a conclusion, often as a basis for action. With any project, such as creating and planning a mindfulness course, the rational mind is essential. Most of us have a well-developed rational mind as this is encouraged in our culture.

Intuitive knowing is a different kind of knowing, which is generally less trusted. It is not a linear process; it doesn't happen in time but is felt in the moment. It isn't rational or analytical, but an instinctive, holistic response to a question or situation. It may not always turn out to be 'right', but that is not the best way of looking at it. Right and wrong belong to the rational mind. Our intuition communicates to us via felt senses, quiet whispers, nudges and flashes; it is felt in the body. There is no set of instructions for accessing it – how we do this will be different for each of us - but for this to happen we need to be in touch with the body.

The following exercise might help in discovering your own intuition:

- Grab a pen and paper.
- Take the pen in your dominant hand and at the top of the page write: *Hello Intuitive Self, how are you today?*
- Then take the pen in your non-dominant hand and write a brief response. Don't think about this, just write a line or two. It may look like a child's writing but that doesn't matter.
- Then keep repeating this procedure, with more questions.

If you get stuck, here are some questions you could ask your intuitive self.

> *Hello Intuitive Self, how are you today?*
> *Are you around much in my life?*
> *It is true to say you are around all the time but I don't always listen?*
> *What is your role or purpose in my life?*
> *How long have you been around in my life?*
> *If I listened to you more, how would my life be?*
> *Where do you live in my body?*
> *Would you like to be around more when I am teaching mindfulness?*
> *If you were around more, how would my teaching change?*
> *How would my response to questions change?*
> *How would my guiding of meditations change?*
> *Is there anything else you would like to say?*

Tuning in to your intuition

Here are a few pointers for opening to and trusting in your intuition:

Take time to open yourself to the atmosphere in the room

One aspect of intuitive teaching is having a sensitivity to the atmosphere in the room. For example, at a particular point in the course your planned structure may have you giving a talk about labelling thoughts, or leading a meditation on sounds. However, if you are tuned in to the room you may sense a heaviness, some frustration, or resistance. Although nothing has been uttered by the students, you sense something. Following your intuition, instead of sticking with the structure you could choose to open the session to the group. You might ask a question, or invite comments and observations. You might touch on how frustrating mindfulness can be, or how sometimes we feel low and believe it's not working. At times like this we need to be able to leave the structure to one side and respond to the immediate reality of the moment by exploring what is in the room. As well as being productive, this can also be thrilling.

Practise pausing when teaching

What helps us to allow the intuition into teaching is to pause. If we don't pause there is a tendency to come from the mind, from what you already know. If we are locked into the mind we will in all likelihood respond to questions and comments in much the same way as we have done before. The answers are ready baked; we just take them out of the oven and give them to our students one after the other. This is often why some teachers get bored with teaching, because if done like this it can become repetitive. There is also the danger that our students' intuition may sense that there is something inauthentic about the teaching or the teacher. Pausing creates a space which allows us to tune in to the other kind of knowing, that sixth sense which is alive and kicking and just waiting to liven things up a little.

Come out of the mind and listen to what is behind the thinking mind

This sixth sense sees things, knows things which the ego mind doesn't see or know. The intuition responds not just to the worded question but to the wider context: the way a person is sitting, the mood of the questioner and the group, the emotion behind the question. It doesn't need to think any of this through; it just instinctively knows.

Intuition is always alive and in the moment, and every moment is different. If we teach intuitively, it's not that we will be teaching something new each time we open our mouths, but that what we say will be a fresh and stimulating expression of it. For example, a student may be talking about an uncomfortable feeling such as anxiety. A conventional thinking-mind response might be to ask them to accept it. But our sixth sense might intuit the student's resistance to such a suggestion and instead prompt us to throw out questions like 'Where in the body do you feel it?', 'What shape is it?' This could possibly jolt the student into a more direct relationship with their feeling of anxiety, opening up a different route to acceptance.

An intuitive response from the teacher may not be immediately understood by the mind of the student, but somewhere inside their intuition will receive it. Whether the student trusts in their intuition is another thing.

Respond to the questioner rather than trying to answer the question

When teachers ask me about the enquiry process, I ask them to see themselves not as giving answers but always as responding to the student. The nature of the response depends on the nature of the question - not just the words, but how it is asked and the context. Responses can take many forms: a shrug of a shoulder; a smile which may say to the student 'You already know the answer to this'; a story or metaphor; silence and a raised eyebrow.

In one of my teaching sessions, a dedicated and delightful female doctor started talking about a particular experience of hers. She went on and on, and was very much in her mind, trying to work it all out; tighter and tighter she wound herself in complexity. I could feel the group getting tense and restless, and my tummy was tightening. Instead of interrupting and stopping her, I put my hands to my tummy and toppled off my meditation cushion onto the floor. The group roared with laughter and so did she. She realised exactly what she had been doing, and let it all go. I hadn't said a word. I didn't think about it at all. It just happened. It was an intuitive response – simple, direct and effective. Of course it was *my* intuitive response, produced by my character; yours would be different.

Keeping it simple, elegant and practical

Intuitive teaching is very much in tune with the three pillars of excellent mindfulness teaching: simplicity, elegance and practicality.

Simplicity is its essence. Intuition knows something and knows it now. It is an immediate sensing of something; it sees things in the moment and responds in the moment. If we can stay in touch with this immediacy, then our teaching is forever new, fresh and simple. Intuition doesn't complicate anything or get caught up in other people's complexity; we complicate things when we are lost in mind. The intuition sees things very simply, and intuitive teaching always brings clarity.

How we respond to a student will be different for each teacher and each situation. One teacher may respond with a rational remark, another with a smile or a joke. However, if we are allowing our intuition to be in the room, then that response will always be simple and immediate. Intuitive teaching comes from the heart and enters the heart of the student. Elegance goes hand in hand with simplicity. Elegant teaching is often achieved by knowing what to leave out, and intuitive teaching instinctively knows what to leave out for maximum benefit. We may say less but it will mean more. We all know the saying: *silence speaks louder than words*. Intuition knows when to be elegant and let the silence speak.

In my dictionary, one of the definitions of elegance is "being pleasantly ingenious and simple". I really like this definition, which points to the imaginative and inventive aspects of elegance. There is a touch of magic about the intuition because it sees things from many different angles. The intuitive part of us is also courageous, and without courage we don't have the conviction to carry through these magical and ingenious responses. If fear is running the show, we will shy away from doing the unusual and the daring, and these approaches can be very effective for our students.

The third pillar of mindfulness teaching is practicality, and in some quarters intuition is regarded as airy and insubstantial, not grounded in real life, floating around in the fuzzy minds of hippies and New Agers. However, this is a mistake. Intuition is very grounded and has nothing to do with having our heads in the clouds. In my dictionary, one of the definitions for practical is "being concerned with the actual doing or use of something rather than with theory and ideas", and that is what we want our mindfulness teaching to be.

Intuitive teaching is about making your teaching relevant to the everyday life of each and every student. Intuitive teaching has no interest in keeping it mystical and other worldly; it is not attracted to theories or philosophies. Its concern is with real life, with the lived, felt experience of being human and all that entails. When we allow intuition to be in the room, we are concerned with keeping mindfulness relevant to a person's life - which includes the self, home, relationships, work, and every activity from chopping vegetables to driving a car. Mindfulness is all about present-moment awareness and what is more practical and grounded than being aware of the present moment? When your thinking mind is tempted to move your teaching into the realms of theories and generalities, intuition will keep you in touch with the essential practicality of mindfulness.

The benefits of intuitive teaching

The teaching which comes from intuition is always alive and fresh because it is not based solely on our bank of knowledge. Teaching which arises out of the intuition is more challenging because it is willing to say what needs saying. It is not trying to please anybody. The intuition is always context-oriented; in other words, it is not solely concerned with ourselves, but has the benefit and welfare of the group at heart.

One of the ways we block our more instinctive teaching is by letting the people- pleaser in us do the teaching. When this happens, the teaching will be there to make our students feel good, so that they like us and we feel good. This is not in anyone's best interests. In Pema Chodron's words: "Instead of offering a friend medicine, bitter though it may be when ingested, you feed them more poison—at the very least, you don't take it away from them." The poison might taste nicer than the medicine, but it does harm instead of helping to heal. She goes on to explain that this sort of teaching is selfish, because you are more concerned with your own feelings than with attending to your friend's (or student's) actual needs.

If we need to please our students, then the teaching will inevitably cease to be challenging and transformative. We need to be willing to disagree, to stimulate and stretch our students. When we teach from the intuition, we are prepared to take ourselves and our students to a place that is new, edgy, just a little uncomfortable - and that is where the growth is. The best fruit is always out on a limb.

This is where intuitive teaching is wonderful. If we are teaching from ego (I don't use that term often but don't have a better one right now) then in all likelihood we will be overly concerned with how we are judged; we will want to be liked, to be seen as a kind teacher. But when we teach from intuition we are willing, though always with kindness, to say things to our students that they need to hear, not what will make them feel better for a little while.

The intuition doesn't suffer from fear so will do what needs to be done, and this is its connection to compassion. True compassion possesses both intelligence and courage; it is willing to cause short term pain to alleviate long term suffering. Intuition does not need to be liked, does not worry about being judged and is not concerned with being seen in a certain way. What intuition is concerned with is doing the best it can and giving the students what they need. This may sometimes be unpleasant, but it is always truly kind and truly compassionate.

When we teach intuitively we don't know what is going to happen next, and this can be uncomfortable for us if we tend to over-rely on the rational mind in our teaching. It may feel risky, but if you can learn to trust your intuition you will find that it can bring huge benefits to both you and your students.

*

I must emphasise, though, that to teach intuitively we do need experience or knowledge of what we are talking about. We cannot just make it up. As we grow in practice and experience as mindfulness teachers, we can develop the confidence to allow intuition to feed naturally into our teaching. Intuition is like a muscle, the more we use it the stronger it becomes.

It's not that when we begin teaching intuitively we throw away the structure of a session or our rational mind. It's rather that our knowledge, experience and intuition knit together and work as a whole. Over time, our teaching becomes a beautiful blend of the rational and the intuitive, a formidable alliance.

11 USING STORIES AND METAPHORS

"The shortest distance between a human being and the truth is a story."

Anthony de Mello

After the eight-week course ends, our students are offered the opportunity to attend our monthly practice evenings and longer retreats, alongside our *Awakening Heart* online programme. Many of them tell us that what they remember most vividly from the eight-week course are the stories and metaphors.

Please don't think I am against conceptual explanations - we couldn't teach without them - but I prefer mixing it up and using a variety of teaching strategies. Metaphors and stories are a magical teaching tool, and time and again I see the impact they can have on students.

Teaching that is mainly focused around concepts can be rather dry, and it is good to remember that although we are intellectual beings, we are also imaginative ones. Stories, metaphors and images reach parts that concepts do not.

Stories

It must come as no surprise that stories can be a part of teaching mindfulness, but I wonder how many of us actually do use them to do that. For some teachers, it can be a little daunting to launch into a story to illustrate a teaching point. But if you practise this, your teaching will evolve onto another level.

If a teacher on one of our courses says to the group, "Let me tell you a story", I see people begin to pay more attention. They lighten up and relax. Everybody enjoys a good story.

The story does need to be told well, so it's a good idea to practise storytelling. When telling a story, I don't exactly put on different voices, but I will change my character a little, or the tone of my voice. It helps if you can embody the characters in the story to some degree, without going over the top.

It also helps if you tell the story in your own words. You are welcome to use any of the stories in this book or my other books, but do try to tell them in your own words if you can. If you feel that you own the story, you will be more at ease and communicate more effectively.

Above all, don't rush through the story; learn to use silence and pauses for effect. And enjoy yourself – if you do, the listeners will.

Texting and nexting

This is a story from my own life. I use this whenever the opportunity arises. It may be part of the students' home practice or it may be a more general illustration of how we rush through life.

One day I was sitting in a traffic jam, when I noticed to my left on the pavement a woman walking along and texting.

Nothing wrong with this of course, and there is no judgment here of the woman, as most of us do this. But what I also noticed was that she was leaning forward and rushing, which again most of us do.

Walking and texting is quite a common sight in most countries nowadays, and may not be a cause for concern. However, maybe because I had nothing else to do, I started to ponder on this. It was not the texting that was most remarkable thing, but the fact that she seemed to be leaning forward, almost leaning forward into the future.

I pondered the word "texting" - a strange word when you repeat it to yourself. But then the word "nexting" came to mind. It occurred to me that the woman was not only texting; she was also nexting. Her attention was not on the here and now, but on what was coming next. She was lost in the future.

Commentary

I think most of us spend much of our time nexting. "Next" implies the future, that which is to come, but is not here yet. If you pay attention and are honest with yourself, you will notice that most of the time you are nexting. When we are not doing this, then often we may be lost in the past.

I don't mean that nexting is wrong or bad or anything like that. What I mean is that a lot of our activities are done because we are incapable of being in the present. We are slaves to doing.

Many people come to me about the cause of stress, and I must say the cause is often very simple. We have too many thoughts in our heads telling us that all sorts of things need doing. These thoughts are constantly pulling us out of the present moment.

This story will be told by one of our teachers or myself, and then we give the students home practice. We ask them, during the course of the following week, to observe when they are nexting, to notice when they are rushing from one thing to another, just skimming across life rather than experiencing it. We ask them also to notice their thoughts and judgments about this, but the main point is to learn to observe themselves when they are nexting.

At the next teaching session, we ask them if they noticed themselves nexting like the woman in the story. Invariably people say yes, and this generates discussion.

What is very clear is that they remember the teaching because it was a story, full of vivid detail - with myself in the car, tapping my steering wheel to music, getting a little bored in the traffic, seeing this woman texting in the street and so forth. Instead of just asking them to notice when they are rushing, telling a story makes the message memorable.

Grandmother mind

This is another story from my own life, which I was prompted to remember when thinking about the Japanese term *sobo maindo*, which means "grandmother mind". In the Mindfulness tradition, our happiness is dependent on developing *sobo maindo*.

I often use this story when speaking around acceptance and welcoming our experience – the pleasant and the unpleasant. But also I may just decide to launch into this and any other story or anecdote for that matter. I find they are always relevant.

When I was a young boy, my Mum used to take me to see my Grandmother. She was always "Gran" to me. My Mum would open the door, I would run in, and my Gran would say, "Come here son," and give me a big kiss. She would open her arms and give me a big cuddle. I used to love going to my Gran's. She may have been the same with all of her grandchildren but I didn't care. I just knew she loved me.

My Mum would sometimes say, "He has been naughty you know. He hasn't washed behind his ears, and he didn't brush his teeth."

But it didn't matter to my Grandmother. She would just say, "I don't care. Come here son and give me a kiss. You go and do your shopping and leave him with me."

Commentary

Just as my Gran welcomed everything about me, so we need to do the same with ourselves. It is not that she would never say to me, "Go and wash, darling," or that she never corrected me when I was naughty. She did, but she loved me anyway.

In our mindfulness practice we need to develop this same attitude. Whatever emotions we may be experiencing - self-criticism, failure, embarrassment, shame, sadness, joy or whatever - we need to meet our experience with grandmother mind.

Grandmother mind is the mind of compassion. It doesn't judge, it doesn't condemn or criticise, it doesn't pick faults or gossip about people. Grandmother mind is open and warm, it welcomes everything into its embrace. Grandmother mind is discerning, but not judgmental.

Often, we turn away from our own difficult emotions. The last thing we want to do is to open our hearts to something we don't like. However, this is the very thing we need to do if we are to stop the inner conflict which causes us so much unhappiness.

When we are experiencing difficult emotions, most of us have a tendency to stay in our heads. We try to work it all out, we try to scheme, but the grandmother mind lives in the heart. If we stay in the head with its stories, opinions, and judgments, we cannot hear the heart and what it is saying.

The heart always welcomes whatever is happening, no matter how much it hurts. As well as being the place of gentleness and welcoming, the heart is the place of courage. If we talk about people who have shown courage in life, we never say they have a brave head, but a brave heart. If we can learn to live in the heart, then we learn to live not only more compassionately but also more courageously. Our Compassion meditation again and again takes us from the abstract world of the head to the real world of the heart and the realm of feeling.

I think this is a wonderful way of conveying the message of acceptance, of turning towards and welcoming all those parts of ourselves which we don't like. We can try to explain it over and over again, but sometimes all we need is a different approach, an approach which touches people's hearts, like a story.

Metaphors

Metaphors are my own personal favourite way of conveying a message. A metaphor, developed in a way that is similar to a story, can cut through and communicate something where a thousand words might fail. A vivid metaphor is intriguing and entertaining, and therefore likely to be more memorable than direct explanation.

I want to offer you some of my favourite metaphors for you to share with your students. Also, I think it is a very good practice to develop your own. They often come unbidden when we have been practising for a while.

Mirror in the bathroom

I often draw on this metaphor when people get caught up with what mindfulness is. For example, a while ago, when I was leading a mindfulness course in a workplace, the woman sitting next to me said that the meditation made her tense in the neck. I checked out the usual postural aspects, but I wanted to go a little deeper with her and the class. I wanted to show her that mindfulness doesn't really do anything to us, so I shared this metaphor with the group.

When you wake up in the morning you go to the bathroom, and on your wall is normally a mirror. We don't always want to look in the mirror as it can be a little disturbing. It can reveal the brutal reality of our facial expression and we often want to turn away from that.

However, the mirror doesn't do anything to us. It just reflects back what is happening, and it never lies. It may show you that you need a shave, or that your mascara has run, or that you have a new spot, or that you look rested from a good sleep.

So, the mirror reflects back what is happening on the outside. It tells us the truth about how we look to other people.

Commentary

Mindfulness is like that mirror. When we sit in meditation we are looking into the mirror of mindfulness. Only this mirror reflects back what is happening on the inside, not the outside. Just like the mirror, it doesn't lie, because mindfulness doesn't make things up.

If we know how to look into the mirror of mindfulness, we see things about ourselves. We notice our habitual thinking patterns and how we are run by our habits. We notice how we treat ourselves and other people. We observe how restless or insecure or unhappy we are. Mindfulness doesn't *do* anything to us, but just reveals what is there. Then, as a consequence, change begins to happen.

Of course, mindfulness may release long-held unacknowledged emotions, which may cause tension for a while, but this is part of the healing that takes place.

In the case of the woman mentioned above, she got it. She realised what I was pointing to and said that she rarely takes a break from the computer, so perhaps that was what was being reflected back to her. It was a lovely moment.

A room with two doors

Sometimes, during a group session on dealing with difficult emotions, I will choose to introduce a meditation on vulnerability. In order to prepare the students for this, I sometimes use the following metaphor.

Imagine there is a room with two doors. One door is always open; the other is quite often closed. Imagine also there is a line of people entering the room through the open door. The people never stop entering, and at some point the room starts to get overcrowded, because people can't get out of the room as fast as they are entering it. More and more people crowd into the room, clogging up all the space. It becomes very claustrophobic. Sooner or later even the walls come under strain. What do you think might eventually happen?

Commentary

As you may have guessed, the room represents ourselves. The open door represents life, and life never stops happening; experiences of all kinds, pleasant and unpleasant, keep crowding in on us. The closed door represents our unwillingness to experience life as it is, in all its aspects, as it happens. I am talking here mainly of the more painful emotions, such as fear, anger, sadness, grief and so on. When we refuse to allow these natural emotions free passage, we close the second door to avoid having to process them. The risk then is that we will be overwhelmed and feel that life is too much.

Mindfulness meditation is not about trying to close the first door so we don't feel anything unpleasant; it is about opening the second door. All experience wants simply to be experienced for a duration and then allowed to pass away. This is healthy, and brings an ease of being and a joy in life.

However, we tend to make a problem out of emotions that seem threatening. We don't like to feel sad, perhaps because we may appear weak, or because it seems to point to something being wrong and life not going our way. So, what we do when they show their little heads is to try and shove them back down again out of sight. We close the door on them and hope they'll disappear in the crowd. If we keep the door closed, at some point the walls of our room will come under strain and – well, we know what might happen next.

We open the second door by turning toward our emotions, allowing them to move through the room and keeping the door open so they can pass on. Sadness, for example, is a natural response to some events in life and can actually season our soul. Sadness breaks open our hearts to allow others to enter. If we close the door on sadness, we remain locked away in our own little experience of life, and experience emotional claustrophobia as a result.

To open the door, we need to notice how we close it; we need to observe how we turn away from painful emotions and allow our thoughts to run rampant. We can then take our attention away from the thoughts and into the felt experience of the emotions in the body. We can see our practice as experiencing opening the second door.

Fiddling with the flowers and standing back

I want to end this chapter with another metaphor which can help explain just what mindfulness is, and which touches on the notions of being and doing. This one is adapted from Charlotte Joko Beck, but it also really did happen at our venue some years ago.

I am sure most of us are familiar with flower arranging. If you have not arranged a vase of flowers yourself, you will at least have seen it done. My wife Gaynor often arranges flowers for the retreats we lead. One particular morning, as I was sitting preparing for a retreat and sipping my cup of Yorkshire tea, I was watching Gaynor arrange the flowers. She would fiddle with them and stand back. She would fiddle a little more and stand back again.

She would do this four or five times, and then, when she was happy with them, she would put them in the meditation space. Now, she had to fiddle with the flowers or else they would not have looked pretty. But what was the point of her standing back? Well, she had to stand back to see how they looked in relation to each other, the vase, and the room. The fiddling is absolutely essential, but so is the standing back. The standing back and just looking gave her a perspective on the flowers that she would not have got if she had just been up close and fiddling with them.

Commentary

When watching Gaynor, I thought what she was doing was a good way of explaining meditation. In life, we have to fiddle; in other words, we have to be active. We have to be in the doing mode some of the time or else nothing would get done. But there are times when we need just to stand back from life.

This is what meditation is about. When we sit in meditation, or indeed when we come back to awareness in daily life, we are in a way standing back from life. We observe ourselves instead of just being lost in doing. So when we sit in meditation for twenty minutes, we get a chance to see our life from a different perspective: one of being and observing, instead of doing. But when we meditate, we are also standing back from something else; we are standing back from our own experience. We are observing our own thoughts and emotions instead of being lost in them.

This illustrates for me the paradox of observing oneself whilst being deeply immersed in the experience. This is why we need to emphasise mindfulness of the body. If we don't, we can easily encourage what my teacher Sangharakshita used to call "alienated awareness". Alienated awareness is when we are out of touch with our own body, feelings and emotions. We are often lost in our head and tend to live out of that. If we are not careful in our teaching, we can encourage this sort of aloofness from our bodies.

Doing yoga, tai chi and other physical activities is of course useful, but that is not what I am talking about here. I have taught some yoga teachers who are very much in touch with their bodies and their feelings and emotions, but I have also seen others who, although they can get into all sorts or shapes and impressive postures, are very much out of touch with their body and feelings.

So when we talk about observing ourselves, we also need to talk about experiencing ourselves, experiencing and feeling our bodies.

12 MORE STORIES AND METAPHORS

"You can't stop the waves, but you can learn to surf."
                                                     Jon Kabat-Zinn

Below are a few more metaphors and stories for your own use. After each I will give a little explanation of its meaning and its relevance for our teaching. However, most are pretty obvious. Remember these are metaphors and stories so they are not factually accurate, and they are not set in stone. You can take stories and metaphors and just play with them; that is part of their magic for teaching.

There are times when I will just tell a story because it is amusing or the moment takes me. The story may not even be relevant to our theme but I tell it anyway. I don't think everything has to have a deeper meaning. We can just have fun, that's meaning enough.

Gulliver's travels

Gulliver was a man who went on a sea journey. He set out in his ship and steered into a storm. He was washed up on the shores of Lilliput. Lilliput was inhabited by thousands of six-inch-high people. As you can imagine, they were terrified of him.

Their aim was to get him, to capture him so they could feel safe. They tried all ways to get him but he was just too strong, too big and too smart. However, they did get him. They got him and tied him up. When did they get him? They got him when he fell asleep.

Commentary

I use this story to illustrate how we need to be aware of our thoughts rather than trying to suppress or get rid of them.

The little six-inch people represent our thoughts - not our useful and conscious thoughts but our chattering minds with their opinions, judgments, criticisms and so on. Like the little people, these chattering thoughts have no power while we are awake and aware, but the moment we fall asleep by losing our awareness they pounce and take us over. We are off. We believe what they tell us until we wake up again.

Noticing our thoughts, labelling them, helps us to wake up out of the stories they tell.

The two arrows

We can see an unfortunate event as like being stabbed by an arrow. It is painful. It is something we don't want in our life. But life brings these challenging events, irrespective of our wishes. The unfortunate event may be the end of a relationship, bad news about a job, a headache, or more serious ill-health. It may also be a criticism or being snubbed by somebody. This is the first arrow. However, the problem is what comes next.

The first arrow enters and hurts us, but then as quick as lightning we reach for a second arrow and stab ourselves with it. The second arrow is the way we think about the first one. We may automatically go into thinking thoughts such as, "I hate this, it always happens to me", or "Nobody understands what I have been through", or "Here we go again – just my rotten luck". We may go over and over the hurt in our heads, working up our emotions, wallowing in our misery, or anger, or resentment, or self-pity, or self-justification, or whatever. We are now suffering the hurt from two arrows, not just one.

Commentary

I use this story to illustrate the difference between pain and suffering, and how we create suffering out of the events of life.

The first arrow comes from outside; it is an event beyond our control. We cannot avoid this event or the hurt it brings with it. But the second arrow is wielded by ourselves; the hurt it produces is entirely self-inflicted. Those thoughts and judgments and opinions that we allow to take us over don't help at all; they only cloud the issue and make it more difficult for us to deal with the real hurt caused by the first arrow.

This doesn't mean that we shouldn't think about the situation; of course we need to assess the damage done by the event that couldn't be avoided. But there is a big difference between having uncontrolled thoughts that don't get us anywhere except for making us feel worse, and thinking to oneself, "So what do I need to do about this?" or something similar. It is the dwelling on, the ruminating which is the problem; this is the second arrow.

Through awareness, we can learn to see ourselves doing this. And then we will be able to put down the second arrow and give ourselves a clearer view of the actual hurt or pain we have experienced.

The seventy-seven problems

Once, a farmer went to tell the Buddha about his problems. He described his troubles with his family. His wife was ill, his children misbehaved and his brother would not help him. He told the Buddha about his harvest, which was sometimes plentiful, but sometimes all washed away by the rains. He described how he felt frustrated most of the time and worried for his family. After all this, he asked how the Buddha could help him with his problems.

"I am sorry," the Buddha said, "but I cannot help you."

"Then what is the point of your teaching, if you cannot help me?"

The Buddha replied, "Sir we all have seventy-seven problems. Of course a few will go, but others will soon take their place. You will always have seventy-seven problems."

"So you cannot help me?" the man said angrily.

"I cannot help you with the seventy-seven problems, but I can help you with the seventy- eighth problem," replied the Buddha.

"The seventy-eighth problem - what is that?"

The Buddha replied, "Sir, the seventy-eighth problem is that you think you shouldn't have any problems."

Commentary

I use this story to illustrate that it is our expectations and demands of life which are the problem, not life itself. If we are honest enough, we will have to admit that we believe our lives should be free from problems, and from anything that disturbs us.

We come to our practice believing that mindfulness, or if you like, a spiritual practice, will solve our problems. But a life of awareness is not about having a problem-free life; that is impossible. Our practice is about realising who we are, ending or at least diminishing our suffering and moving towards happiness. Please don't get hung up on the word "happiness" – it is just one possible term. Some people may prefer to use other terms such as contentment, peace of mind, lack of anxiety and so on.

Our relationship to our problems does change as a result of meditation, but things will still happen. The bus will still be late, you will still get criticised, your car will break down and you will become ill and indeed die.

In this story you can change the Buddha figure for a meditation master or teacher if you wish.

Who's this in the shower with me?

This is a story from my own life.

A few years ago, I had a small wager with a friend that Chelsea would win the Champions' League. After all, they had one of the best managers in the world in Jose Mourinho. One particular match, they were playing at home. They lost the match. They were out of the Champions' League. They had lost at home in the Champions' League.

The next morning, I was having a shower, and lo and behold the then Chelsea manager Jose Mourinho turns up uninvited into my shower. I prefer to shower alone of course, but there you go.

I started telling him off. "How could you lose at home to a side from Spain which had ten men? The team were useless." I told him where he had gone wrong and how he should have approached the game.

Then BING! I realised what I was doing. Jose Mourinho hadn't entered the shower uninvited; I had invited him in. I let him leave, and then decided that while I was in the shower I might as well have one.

Commentary

I use this story to illustrate that often we are doing one thing with the body but something else with the mind.

How often are we carrying out an activity only to find we are mentally engaged in a different one? Living a mindful life is the beginning of noticing this and learning to be present with what we are doing. The present moment is where we eventually find the joy we have been searching for all our lives.

On the courses I run I ask people, just as you will of your students, to notice when they are engaged in everyday activities like drinking coffee, walking up the stairs and doing the washing up, and to notice just how often they drift away. They soon come to realise that even though they are washing the dishes with their body, their mind is doing something else. For some this can come as quite a surprise at just how much unnecessary thinking goes on.

The river

> You have been telling the people that this is the Eleventh Hour.
> Now you must go back and tell the people that this is The Hour.
>
> Here are the things that must be considered:
> Where are you living?
> What are you doing?
> What are your relationships?
> Are you in right relation?
> Where is your water?
> Know your garden.
> It is time to speak your Truth.
> Create your community.
> Be good to each other.
> And do not look outside yourself for the leader.
>
> This could be a good time!
> There is a river flowing now very fast.
> It is so great and swift that there are those who will be afraid.
> They will try to hold on to the shore.
> They will feel like they are being torn apart, and they will suffer greatly.

Know the river has its destination.
The elders say we must let go of the shore, push off toward the middle of the river,
Keep our eyes open, and our heads above the water.

See who is there with you and celebrate.
At this time in history we are to take nothing personally, least of all ourselves!
For the moment we do, our spiritual growth and journey comes to a halt.
The time of the lonely wolf is over.
Gather yourselves!
Banish the word "struggle" from your attitude and vocabulary.
All that we do now must be done in a sacred manner and in celebration.
We are the ones we have been waiting for.

Commentary

This story or poetic teaching is from the Elders of the Hopi tribe in Arizona. I use it for many reasons. You can read it over and over again; there is much material to explore here.

The main reason I use it is to show how clinging leads to suffering. The sentence *"They will try to hold on to the shore"* stands out for me. We try to hold on. We hold on to possessions, people, jobs and reputations. We hold on to ideas, beliefs, opinions and a sense of identity. We hold on for dear life, and it only creates suffering.

We get battered by the river of life if we try to hold on to the shore. Life has to keep moving, but in our desperation we refuse again and again, out of fear, to let go of our habitual tendencies.

After reading this out, I often ask the group if they have any comments, and what it is that they cling to in their lives.

The meditation master and the cleaning lady

Hakuin the meditation master is ninety years old and he decides to visit his old friend Basho in the next valley. Basho is also ninety years old. They have been friends since they were eight years old. They entered monastic life together as children and trained together for decades.

He gathers all his monks and nuns together and tells them that he intends to go and see his dear old friend Basho. He explains that neither of them has long to live and it is time for them to see each other one last time. He asks them all to look after each other in his absence and to practise well.

Hakuin and Basho have a wonderful time together, reminiscing and joking, but all things must end and eventually it is time for Hakuin to head back to his own monastery.

Hakuin has a very devoted cleaning lady. Though he can be very stern when he needs to be, Hakuin has always been very kind to her and her family. She loves him very much.

She knows that Hakuin is due back and thinks to herself that she wants to prepare his room for his arrival. She sweeps the floor, cleans his worktops, polishes his ornaments. Then she sees his favourite vase. This vase has been handed down by his master and the masters before him. It is very precious indeed. Each morning after his meditation Hakuin caresses the vase and remembers his beloved masters.

She picks up the vase, begins cleaning it and then drops it. It smashes into a hundred pieces. At that moment, the handle of the door to the room begins to move. Hakuin walks in and she looks at him in horror, ready to apologise.

However, he looks her in the eyes and says, "Don't you worry, my dear. I got that vase for pleasure, not for pain." Then sits her down and makes her a cup of tea.

Commentary

This is one of my favourite stories, and I use it to explore our attitudes to the things we possess. I spent five years with very few possessions whilst living in a Buddhist retreat centre, and I must say I was very happy indeed. I rarely missed the THINGS of this world.

But recently I noticed how irritated I was becoming with our new printer, which seemed incapable of doing the most basic of things, like printing. This got me thinking about my current relationship to my possessions.

One of my reflections was that it is not really possessions that matter, but our relationship to them. Maybe we could all ponder on our relationship to our own possessions. Maybe it is worth asking: do my possessions bring me pleasure or do they bring me pain? Perhaps we can learn to be happy with possessions and happy without them.

Another question to ponder is: why was the master able to respond in this way? There are a few reasons, and it is worth exploring these with the group.

I sometimes blend this story with "A crack in it", which you can find in the "Guiding meditations" chapter. These stories can go well together when exploring vulnerability and pain, or how suffering results from clinging.

The drunk and the moon

A drunk and his friend were staggering home one night when they stopped at the bridge. They stood chatting for a while.

Then Bill said to Fred, "What's that down there?"

"That's the moon," said Fred.

Bill looked again, shook his head in disbelief, and said, "I don't understand. How on earth did I get way up here?"

Commentary

I use this to convey that we almost never see reality. What we tend to see is a reflection of it in the form of words, concepts, opinions, judgments, fears and desires, which we then proceed to take for reality. We always see the world from our own self-centred viewpoint, which invariably leads to suffering and distress.

I like little parables like this one; they have a meaning but their joy is in just being amusing.

Johnny and the biscuit tin

Johnny's mum noticed a biscuit had gone out of the biscuit tin, and only Johnny could have taken it.

His Mum asks, "Johnny, when you were taking a biscuit out of the biscuit tin, did you know that God was watching?"

Johnny replies, "Yes Mum, I did."

"And what did he say?" she asks.

"Take two, nobody is watching," Johnny replied.

Commentary

Like the previous jokey little anecdote, this can illustrate that things are not always what they seem.

More important than any message, though, is that it is funny, and I like it and students do too. Often, I just drop in these little stories at unexpected times.

Bursting balloons

A few years ago, I was at birthday party and noticed that one of the entertainers was blowing up balloons. He would let the children burst the balloon, then instantly he would blow up another. Again they would burst the balloon, and again he would blow up another. The children enjoyed bursting the man's balloons. Each time they did this he would pretend to be disappointed and surprised. But even though he had lots of experience and it was his job to entertain the children, I am sure it was tiring forever blowing up balloons.

Commentary

This image came to me, as they often do, years later during a silent retreat. We are just like the entertainer at the party; most of the day we are blowing up our balloons. Our balloons are full of expectations and demands of our own, and those of other people, situations and life. We blow up our balloons with demands such as: everybody should like me; people should do I want them to do; life needs to go my way; I need to be right; I need to be noticed – and so on. The list is endless.

Life keeps bursting our balloons - because people will not always be nice, you cannot always be right and so on. But rather than learning from the disappointment, we instantly blow up another balloon full of expectations and demands. All day long, bursting and blowing, bursting and blowing - it is exhausting. Life is meant to burst our balloon, it will always attempt to bring us back to reality – no balloon.

It is good to know what demands you are blowing into your balloons. To paraphrase Charlotte Joko Beck, disappointment and deflation can be a wonderful teacher. At least if we recognise our expectations we can try to hold them more lightly.

The path of mindfulness is learning that life is king and will always win in the end. For many of us it takes years to realise this, but when we cease blowing up our balloons, then we begin to taste the real joy of genuinely living here and now with life as it is.

*

If you are interested in reading more stories and metaphors then you can find plenty more in my own book, *A Mindful Life: Who's this in the Shower with me?* and also in Ajahn Brahm's *Who Ordered This Truckload of Dung? Inspiring Stories for Welcoming Life's Difficulties.*

13   AN EIGHT-WEEK COURSE IN MINDFULNESS AND COMPASSION

"Awareness is our true self; it's what we are. So, we don't have to try to develop awareness; we simply need to notice how we block awareness, with our thoughts, our fantasies, our opinions, and our judgments."

Charlotte Joko Beck

I want to finish by sharing our eight-week course in brief. This is our first-level course, aimed at students new to mindfulness. However, we do get people returning to complete it a number of times, and also people who are experienced and are attracted our approach. We also use this course on our teacher training programme, and train our student teachers through it. I am just going to share the essence here; if you would like more information, then just email me.

    Though we have themes for each of the eight sessions, one course can be very different from another. We are flexible, and we want to work with what is in the room rather than sticking with a curriculum. However, this is the basic outline.

Week 1 Mindfulness - the jewel in the ice

We often begin the course with a short silence and introduce mindfulness that way. We don't tell people we are going to be silent, but the teacher will just fall silent and students tend to follow. After a minute or so we will then ask people what they noticed during that silence. There are a number of responses, as you might guess, and then we tell them that they have already been introduced to mindfulness. They have begun to observe their experience, and that is before we have mentioned the word "mindfulness". So we begin with an experience of mindfulness rather than a technical explanation.

Theme and teaching

We explore what mindfulness is and is not, through the metaphor of mindfulness as "the jewel in the ice". We introduce students to the concept of thought labelling as a strategy. We describe our habit of "nexting".

There is enquiry, and also open discussion about whatever anybody has on their mind regarding anything they have read or any assumptions they might have about what practice involves. I find that is a good way to unearth any wrong views that might be lodged in their minds.

Meditation

We focus on the Mindfulness of Breath meditation, taking about fifteen minutes for it. We aim to guide students through this twice during the session, once near the beginning and again towards the end.

Home Practice

We ask the students to try to do at least ten minutes of meditation each day, fifteen if possible, remembering to label their thoughts. We give them access to our *Awakening Heart* programme with several guided meditations on it.

We ask them to begin to bring mindfulness into a few of their daily activities such as having a shower, drinking tea or brushing teeth. We ask them to experience these activities, but also, from Week 1, to notice what it is that takes them away from these activities.

We ask them to try to become aware of when they are nexting.

Week 2   The feeling body

A couple of minutes of silence.

Review

After the silence, we usually begin with a review of home practice, and enquiry. Sometimes, if the mood seems right, we may start with a meditation, followed by the review. The flow of the evenings is very organic.

Theme and teaching

The main theme of this week is about living in the body and the body being our home. The session is really about learning to see what takes us away from our present-moment experience.

This week we also often give the first brief introduction to kindness or compassion. Either this week or in Week 3 we will go into the parable of the two arrows. There is enquiry and discussion where appropriate.

Meditation

The first meditation is the basic Mindfulness of Breath. The second is what most people call the Body Scan but we call the Being at Home meditation; we take around twenty minutes for it.

Home Practice

We ask them to continue with all their home practice from last week. As well as a daily meditation practice, we ask them again to pay attention to what takes them away from brushing their teeth, drinking tea and walking from one room to another.

We mention nexting again and ask people to notice when they are doing it, and to remember to use thought labelling.

If "The two arrows" was covered in the session, we ask them to look out for this and to observe when they find themselves using the second one.

Week 3   Living in the present moment

A couple of minutes of silence.

Review

As with last week, we may begin with a review of home practice, or we may have a meditation followed by the review. If I am leading, I often throw it open and ask if there is anything on people's minds about their practice. I may ask about obstacles and resistance to practice. If not much comes back I may ask them a question: so what's the point of this - it's boring isn't it? If I leave a long enough pause, someone will always speak up; pauses encourage people to speak.

Theme and teaching

The theme for Week 3 builds on Week 2. We talk about what it means to live in the present moment and how to actually do it. We emphasise again that the practice is noticing what takes us away from the present activity.

We speak about taking mindfulness into more areas of our lives: for example, a situation where we are speaking to a work colleague we find difficult, or one we like. We are encouraging students to become a little more aware of their dealings with people and their reactions to them.

This week I may introduce the teaching on the difference between true emotion and false emotion. True emotion has its source in real life events, and false emotion has our unconscious thoughts as its source. This involves a further exploration of the two arrows.

Meditation

The first meditation will be either Mindfulness of Breath or Being at Home. This week we introduce the idea of pausing in everyday life, and practice it several times during the session.

Mindful movement or mindful walking may also be part of the session.

Home Practice

We begin to extend their home practice now. We ask them to practise pausing several times a day. We ask them to observe themselves during what we call the in-between times: for example, when walking from one room to another, or when waiting for something. It is often in these in-between times that we get invaded by thoughts.

We suggest they begin to notice when they are caught in strong emotion and to label their thoughts. When they do this they are then in a position to see if it is false or true emotion. This skill takes time but is so worth the effort put in.

Week 4   Calming the chattering mind

A couple of minutes of silence.

Review

Review normally includes a few more observations around the two arrows, and comments around pausing. I may prompt people to discuss any observations about mindful walking either formally or informally. I will also ask for more general questions or comments around practice and the course material. I may also cover nexting again if it seems appropriate.

By Week 4, students tend to be getting a clearer idea of what we are actually doing. They can realise at this point that we are not involved in self-improvement and it's not a course in positive thinking.

I will review the previous three sessions, and then open it out for comments and observations.

Theme and teaching

Week 4 includes deeper exploration of thought labelling. We also introduce the technique of counting thoughts. This comes from the Tibetan Buddhist tradition. It means that during the day, when we find we are lost in lots of thinking, we simply pause and count how many thoughts we are having. Bringing direct attention to thoughts in this way tends to stop or slow them down and to give us some headspace.

However, these techniques are just that - techniques. They can give us respite for a few moments, but they will not result in the deeper changes which we desire. Those changes only come after many months and years of good practice.

We also offer a few other techniques for use in daily life. We show people how to lengthen their out-breath by a second or two. This encourages us to take our attention away from our thoughts and into the body and the present moment.

One theme for this session is to begin to bring mindfulness to our interactions with others. We ask people to begin to observe themselves when wanting approval from somebody. This could be a boss, a spouse or a work colleague. Non-judgmental awareness has been explained and now students are getting a sense of how to observe themselves without criticism or judgment, or at least how to observe that too.

Another area is saying yes when really wanting to say no. In my view, the ability to say no is one of the biggest stress busters there is. We need to develop the ability to say no when we want to say no. A lot of us are pleasers, which can lead to overload and stress and often develop into resentment, which then leads to a busy mind. How we are and what we do impacts on how we think, and vice versa.

Either this week or in Week 5, we talk about the four truths of life. This is taking mindfulness back its roots in Buddhism. I am not going to give a deep explanation here of the four truths as it is not the place for it. If you wish, you can read Ajahn Sumedho's short book *The Four Noble Truths* which explains them wonderfully.

The Buddha identified mindfulness as the primary way of bringing suffering to an end, along with a lifestyle that is conducive to the practice of it. This is often one of the most interesting themes we cover, as it normalises distress. It illustrates that we all suffer and we are not alone, and shows each and every student that a happier life is within their own grasp.

We talk about seeing mindfulness as a golden thread. When we are in awareness, so to speak, we have hold of the golden thread of mindfulness. This doesn't mean that life will go better or be different, but at least we are here with life whilst it is happening.

The thread is golden because it is precious; after all, when we are not aware we are not present with life. Inevitably we will drop the golden thread again and again for the rest of our lives, but the moment we realise that we have dropped it, we are holding it once again. We don't need to go searching for it and we don't need to criticise ourselves for dropping it; that would be more of the same old tired way of being. We simply need to note where we have been, what stories we have been entertaining, and come back again to the golden thread.

Meditation

This week we practise both the Mindfulness of Breathing and the Being at Home meditation.

During the Mindfulness of Breathing, I may introduce counting the breaths, which most teachers will be familiar with. This means just dropping a count of one at the end of the first out-breath, then two after the next one and so on up to ten, and then starting again from one. This can help to just gather our attention for a while at the beginning of a meditation or during it. Alternatively - and this is why I like the course to be flexible - I may ask students to be aware of the end of the out-breath. There is a natural letting go there, so we can tune in to that.

I don't want to introduce too many different meditations, as it is better for students to deepen their understanding of one or two rather than to practise many and not understand any.

Home Practice

As well as meditations, we suggest that students move from choosing from a few mindful activities to including more and more of their lives. We ask them not as a way of striving but with the analogy of the golden thread.

We also ask students to carry on with pausing as a way of resetting, or recollecting themselves throughout the day.

We ask them to notice when they nod in agreement with somebody when in their heart they don't agree. Bringing attention to this can be very revealing; we may see that we do this to be liked, or that we are afraid of being disapproved of if we disagree with somebody. If we do this over the long term then we disconnect from our own heart and indeed from trusting in our heart.

Week 5   Dancing with dragons

A couple of minutes of silence.

Review

We often start off with either a meditation or discussing the golden thread. We may cover a little more of the four truths. However, because we don't always stick to a strict programme we are always free just to respond to what is in the room. I may sense a heaviness or tiredness and may start with a few words about that.

Theme and teaching

Everybody who comes through the door of a meditation course attends the course to change something about themselves, but if we don't know how change happens we can get off on the wrong foot and develop an unhelpful attitude to practice. This is where we return to our original metaphor at the start of the course. We re-emphasise that mindfulness is like the sun; it melts the "ice" of our habitual tendencies.

The teaching in this session is about developing the observing self: that aspect of ourselves that has the capacity to notice and observe the drama without getting involved in it. That is one aspect of it. However, we also need to experience the bodily counterpart of that habitual tendency. For example, I may have a tendency to withdraw whenever there is difficult communication with another. Now, I could glean information about this, perhaps through therapy; I might realise that it was to do with a particular aspect of my upbringing, which it will be anyway. However, information is not enough; what I need to do is to experience the bodily counterpart, the withdrawing in the body. These strategies, these habitual tendencies over the decades, get trapped into the very cells of the body, and that is where I need to go to resolve them.

So we ask people both to observe their thoughts about the situation and to experience the contraction in the body. Observing and experiencing are the keys to freedom. We point out that we change via these two qualities, and not by *trying* to change. The sun doesn't *try* to melt the ice; it just happens.

At some point during this session, we suggest working with one upset per day, and give this as home practice.

Meditation

The first meditation during this session is either the Mindfulness of Breathing or the Being at Home meditation. We then practice what I call the Dancing with Dragons meditation. This is sometimes called Working with Difficulties or Untying Emotional Knots, but I prefer the more mythical name as it also feeds into the teaching around the practice.

Students can access these guided meditations on our *Awakening Heart* programme.

Home Practice

We ask students to practice both the Mindfulness of Breath and the Dancing with Dragons meditations.

Part of the teaching this week is about learning to work with upset during the day, so part of home practice is asking people to learn to recognise upset in its many forms and be able to work with it. We show them how to do it in the moment and also after the event if we miss it, as we often do.

We also ask them to continue with the regular mindful activities. At this point, if I think it appropriate for the group, I may suggest they begin to bring awareness to waking up in the morning and welcoming any feelings and moods they wake up with.

I think what we have to watch out for at this stage is that students feel overwhelmed with more and more home practice. I like to simplify it by saying something like: your whole life is your practice, but when you miss the opportunity it doesn't matter at all. You just pick up the thread when you remember.

Week 6   The ABC of mindfulness

A couple of minutes of silence.

Review

The review this week is interesting as we invariably discuss working with upset, which can take a bit of getting familiar with. A lot of people think that if they practise mindfulness they won't get upset, so it often comes as a surprise when we ask them to work with upset.

Theme and teaching

The main theme this week is the ABC of mindfulness. I shall not go into detail here about how the theme is presented, as it is not easily explained in a few words. There is a video on our YouTube channel in which I present this teaching, and it is also covered in detail in my book *Mindfulness and Compassion*. Do go to one of those sources to learn about this very useful teaching and how it is put across.

This session is aimed at shifting people's understanding of their own identity, and it is often the week when people's understanding can really change and deepen. It can also leave them a little stunned as they don't quite know what to make of it.

One of the aims of the session is to encourage people to trust in their awareness rather than in their analytical mind. We tend to over-identify with our thoughts and our self-image, and overlook the ever-present awareness in which these thoughts and ideas appear. Earlier in this book we described the thinking mind as a tool, and the "clicky pen" metaphor demonstrated that it is a wonderful tool if used wisely. Our practice can help us to use the mind more wisely.

Meditation

We do a Mindfulness of Breath or a Being at Home meditation.

After teaching the ABC of Mindfulness, we also bring in Just Sitting, sometimes called Choiceless Awareness. Just Sitting is exactly that; it is just sitting and observing what enters into your field of awareness. As we observe over and again we come to understand that all experience is fleeting and changing.

Home Practice

We don't normally bring in anything new at this stage but just consolidate what we are continually aiming to do, which is to establish a regular meditation practice and to learn to bring awareness into everyday life.

We will remind students of the pausing and walking meditations, and discuss more around mindfulness in daily life.

Week 7   Compassion

A couple of minutes of silence.

Review

This week's review can be interesting as people often report the ABC as being a significant session in terms of developing their understanding of how to practise and what happens over time as we practise.

Theme and teaching

We explore how self-compassion and kindness begin with our noticing how and when we are unkind to ourselves: how we talk to ourselves, the tone of thought we use, and so on. We discuss self-care and explore how to look after ourselves during each and every day.

We also look at the difference between true compassion and idiot compassion, true compassion being a genuine response to another's suffering and idiot compassion being a kind of niceness. Idiot compassion is often about wanting to please people and to be liked; true compassion is the willingness to do what is necessary to wake a person up out of their suffering, which initially might be painful for them.

Meditation

Early in the session we do a Being at Home or a Mindfulness of Breath meditation, just to consolidate that practice.

We have talked about self-compassion all the way through the course, and now we bring in the Compassion meditation practice. This practice traditionally has five stages: compassion towards self, towards a friend, towards a neutral person, towards a difficult person and towards all beings. We usually begin with just the first three stages, and then at the end we might briefly bring in the last two.

The best way to view this practice is like planting seeds; we are not expecting to feel compassion right now but are planting seeds for the future. It does not matter what you feel right now – the important thing is just to do the practice.

Home Practice

Having recapped on the two arrows and the golden thread, we ask people over the following week to identify areas in their lives where they find it difficult to maintain awareness of themselves - such as meetings, challenging communications, eating a meal and so on. They can then decide to use these areas to develop their practice.

We ask them to practise the Compassion meditation, which is on the *Awakening Heart* programme, and also to keep doing the Mindfulness of Breath.

Week 8   Bringing mindfulness to life - and what next?

A couple of minutes of silence.

Review

Here we recap on last week and ask them about their experience of compassion meditation. Some really like it and others just don't want to do it. I don't push, but explain that it is very easy to try too hard with this practice by trying to squeeze out compassion for people. I talk about compassion meditation as another way of melting the ice we spoke of in the first week.

Theme and teaching

We explore what it means to live a mindful life. We begin to break it down into small parts: noticing what takes us away from chopping a carrot, from washing up, from tying our shoe laces and zipping up our jacket. These are the minor activities which make up a life, and we show our students how to be present with these activities.

I then recap briefly on each week of the course, and take any questions.

Meditation

I may open it out and ask if there is a request for a particular meditation, or if I think it necessary I will do another Compassion meditation. If a student opts for a different practice we will do that, and then end the whole course on a very short Compassion meditation wishing the whole group well.

Home Practice

As this is the final session of the course, we outline the ways in which we can help in maintaining and developing their mindfulness practice. We suggest they sit daily, and invite them to come along to our practice evenings once a month if they live nearby, to help maintain their practice.

Once a month we run meditation evenings which anybody who has been on a course can attend. These are broadcast live via webinar, so anybody anywhere in the world can join in. They are also recorded for the benefit of those in different time zones.

If people live at a distance or abroad, we offer them membership of the *Awakening Heart* online programme.

We run one-day and weekend retreats periodically throughout the year, as well as week-long silent retreats in the UK, Italy and Spain for those who want to attend a more in-depth retreat.

We also run sesshins (silent meditation days) which are our most popular events. These are by invitation only for those who we think are ready for it. These are in complete silence apart from a little teaching from myself.

For those who want to teach mindfulness, we run teacher training retreats. Normally we expect applicants to have been practising for at least a year. However, we speak to anybody who wishes to attend and assess whether they are ready.

Further resources

Books

Ajahn Brahm: *Who Ordered This Truckload of Dung? Inspiring Stories for Welcoming Life's Difficulties*

Ajahn Sumedho: *The Sound of Silence*

Ajahn Sumedho: *The Four Noble Truths*

Anthony de Mello: *Awareness*

Charlotte Joko Beck: *Nothing Special: Living Zen*

Charlotte Joko Beck: *Everyday Zen: Life and Work*

Chogyam Trungpa: *Cutting Through Spiritual Materialism*

Jon Kabat-Zinn: *Wherever You Go, There You Are: Mindfulness Meditation for Everyday Life*

Pema Chodron: *The Places that Scare You: A Guide to Fearlessness*

Rigdzin Shikpo: *Openness Clarity Sensitivity*

Shunryu Suzuki: *Zen Mind, Beginners Mind*

Sonia Choquette: *Trust Your Vibes*

Steve Hagen: *Buddhism Plain and Simple*

Suryacitta (The Happy Buddha): *Happiness and How it Happens: Finding Contentment Through Mindfulness*

Suryacitta (The Happy Buddha): *Mindfulness and Compassion: Embracing Life with Loving-Kindness*

Suryacitta (The Happy Buddha): *A Mindful Life: Who's this in the shower with me?*

Thich Nhat Hanh: *The Miracle of Mindfulness*

Online

Awakening Heart - online programme for student and teachers:
https://www.mindfulnesscic.co.uk/become-a-member/

Acknowledgement

Above all others involved in the creation of this book I would like to thank Sue my editor. Sue crafted this book from a chaotic collection of thoughts and reflections into the form you see now. She not only crafted but also donated invaluable suggestions and was absolutely key in bringing this to completion. She was brilliant, perceptive and kind. Thank you, Sue.

If you want to contact Suryacitta

Websites
www.mindfulnesscic.co.uk
www.suryacitta.com

Email
suryacitta@gmail.com

Printed in Great Britain
by Amazon